The *Informazing* Resource Book

·

READING & WRITING
NONFICTION

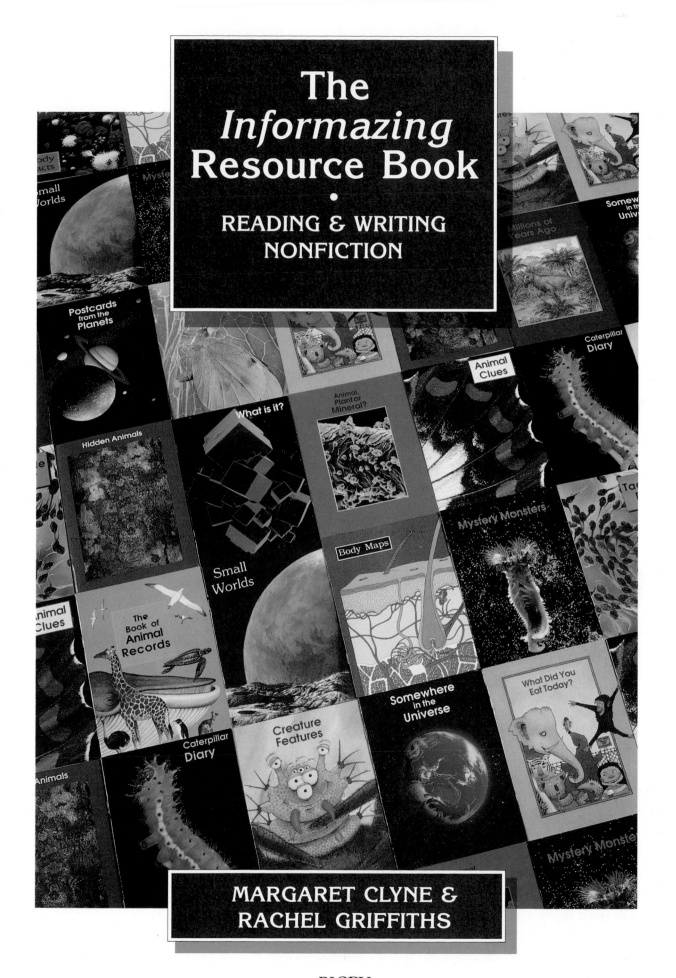

The *Informazing* Resource Book

•

READING & WRITING NONFICTION

MARGARET CLYNE & RACHEL GRIFFITHS

RIGBY

Published by
THOMAS NELSON AUSTRALIA
102 Dodds Street
South Melbourne Victoria 3205

Distributed in the United States of America by
Rigby
A Division of Reed Publishing (USA) Inc
PO Box 797
Crystal Lake IL 60039-0797
800-822-8661

Design by
Black Cockatoo Publishing Pty Ltd
Typeset by Midland Typesetters, Maryborough Australia
Printed in Hong Kong
ISBN 0 7327 0483 9

10 9 8 7 6 5 4 3 2
95 94 93

Informazing big
books can be read
for pleasure as well
as for research.
Children should be
given time to reread
their favorites.

Acknowledgements

Thank you to the teachers and children of Bayview Primary
School, Canterbury Primary School, Donvale Primary School,
Kerrimuir Primary School, Kew Primary School, Milgate Primary
School, Scoresby Heights Primary School, St Anthony's
Glenhuntly, Syndal South Primary School and Waverley North
Primary School.

Thanks also to Elaine Wall, Willard School, Evanston IL, and Mike
Baginski, Main Street School, Montpelier VT.

The book was read in proofs by Bob Scholl, Beth Sycamore,
Penny Trafton and Patty Whitehouse.

Thank you to Steve Moline for his listening, his reading, his
comments, his suggestions and his sense of humor.

Thank you to Lyn Hosking for unravelling the mysteries of
computers and for assisting with the introduction.

Illustration acknowledgements

Classroom photographs by David Heath, John Holmstrom, Steve
Moline and Beth Sycamore. Photographs of children's work by
Steve Moline and David Wallace.

Cover photograph by David Wallace.

Worksheet illustrations in Part 3 by Suzanne Lollback and Kay
Peacock.

The World Map on page 122 is derived from the Outline Map
Series © 1990 Reprinted courtesy of Rand McNally, R.L. 90-S-165.

The photograph on page 60 is reproduced with permission of
Malvern Caulfield Progress (Leader Newspaper Group).

Illustrations and photographs reproduced from the *Informazing*
books themselves:

Ester Kasepuu: 23 (skulls and teeth), 83 (arms and legs, cover).
Dorothy Dunphy: 31 (cover, age of amphibians), 59 (cover, blue
whale), diagrams (73, 76, 77, 79, 80), 99 (galaxy), 111 (craters).
Kathie Atkinson: 35 (cover, dragonfly), 47 (cover, frog), 48,
(crab, grasshopper), 79 (tadpoles, frieze, cover), 80 (frog).
R. and D. Keller/ANT: 38 (gecko).
Otto Rogge/ANT: 40 (fish).
H. and J. Beste/Auscape: 41 (grasshopper).
Mary Davy: 50 (*Creature Features*).
Rob Roennfeldt: 56 (*I Spy*).
M. F. Soper/ANT: 59 (elephant).
Terry Denton: 63, 65 (*What Did You Eat Today?*).
Penny Martin: 66, 67, 69 (diagrams).
NHPA/ANT: 43 (*Skeletons* cover), 67 (lacewing, tree frog, cover
Animal Acrobats), 69 (swallow).
J. and A. Six/Auscape: 73 (butterflies, cover *The Life of the
Butterfly*).
David Maitland/Auscape: 75 (caterpillars, cover *Caterpillar
Diary*).
Horizon/Science Photo Library: 87–89 (*Body Facts*), 91–93
(*Animal Plant or Mineral?*), 95–97 (*What Is It?*), 99 (cover),
103–105 (*Postcards from the Planets*), 107 (*The Gas Giants*),
110–111 (*Small Worlds*), 113 (smokestacks, ozone holes,
rainforest, desert, traffic, cover).
Donna Rawlins: 99 (streetscape), 101 (aerial view).
Mike Gorman: 107 (silhouettes), 110 (block diagram), 113
(ozone layer), 114 (diagrams, map), 115 (map).
Peter Gouldthorpe: 109 (rings of petrol), 110 (Venus landscape),
111 (Mercury landscape).
Weldon Trannies: 113 (cleared rainforest).
J. P. Ferrero/Auscape: 8, 39 (cover *Hidden Animals*).

Dedication

R. G. To Morwenna, always "full of 'satiable curtiosity.'"

M. C. To Steve Moline who made it possible.

Contents

The Informazing classroom • 6

What is Informazing? • 8

Overview charts • 12

Part 1: Reading and writing nonfiction

Chapter 1
Informazing: Learning and teaching

Children are actively involved • 18

Children learn from direct experiences • 18

Children learn from each other • 18

Children make connections across subject areas • 19

Children are able to experiment • 19

Conclusion • 19

Chapter 2
Reading and writing across the curriculum

Reading • 20

Writing • 20

Transferring information into another style or form • 20

Presenting new information in another style or form • 21

Working with nonfiction conventions • 21

Talking • 21

Taking time to talk using the big books • 21

Children talking about their work • 22

The science program • 23

Observing • 23

Experimenting • 24

Classifying • 24

Mathematics: measuring, calculating and comparing • 24

Arts and crafts • 24

Problem solving, puzzles and games • 24

Reading the book and solving the puzzles • 25

Making up puzzles • 25

Research • 26

Constructing questions • 26

Sources of information • 26

"Is that really true?" • 26

Involving families • 27

Chapter 3
Classroom organization

Access to books • 27

Evaluation • 27

Evaluating oral language • 28

Observing children • 28

Work samples • 28

Part 2: Working with Informazing

Chapter 4
Prehistory

Millions of Years Ago • 30

Chapter 5
Animal puzzles

Mystery Monsters • 34

Hidden Animals • 38

Skeletons • 42

Chapter 6
More animal puzzles

Animal Clues • 46

Creature Features • 50

I Spy • 54

Chapter 7
Animal facts

The Book of Animal Records • 58

What Did You Eat Today? • 62

Animal Acrobats • 66

Chapter 8
Life cycles
The Life of the Butterfly ● 70
Caterpillar Diary ● 74
Tadpole Diary ● 78

Chapter 9
The body
Body Maps ● 82
Body Facts ● 86

Chapter 10
Puzzles about the physical world
Animal, Plant or Mineral? ● 90
What Is It? ● 94

Chapter 11
Space
Somewhere in the Universe ● 98
Postcards from the Planets ● 102
Small Worlds ● 106
The Gas Giants ● 106

Chapter 12
The future
Earth in Danger ● 112

Part 3: Blackline masters ● 117

Part 4: Index ● 133

The Informazing classroom

Picture a classroom in which the students and teacher are gathered in what we know as a "shared reading" group. Beside the teacher a "big book" is opened and resting on an easel, while next to it is a chart holder. The students are suggesting characteristics in the life cycle of a tadpole, or using text and picture to guess the solution to a problem, while the teacher lists their responses on the chart paper. The lists will later be made into a graph or a diagram by the children. The big book is not a story, but an information big book, illustrating and describing science concepts.

Informazing books are the ideal way to introduce children to the conventions of non-fiction, in the familiar context of shared book experience.

Informazing is dedicated to three tasks:

● To apply the proven, effective strategies of shared reading techniques using big books in the teaching of science topics and scientific inquiry.

● To provide an environment where students become experienced with the conventions of nonfiction.

● To provide support to students in developing information writing skills: using charts, graphs, diagrams, and other ways of presenting information: the skills necessary to participate in the information age.

Shared writing is an important part of using big books. Children can work together to design their own charts and to edit each other's contributions.

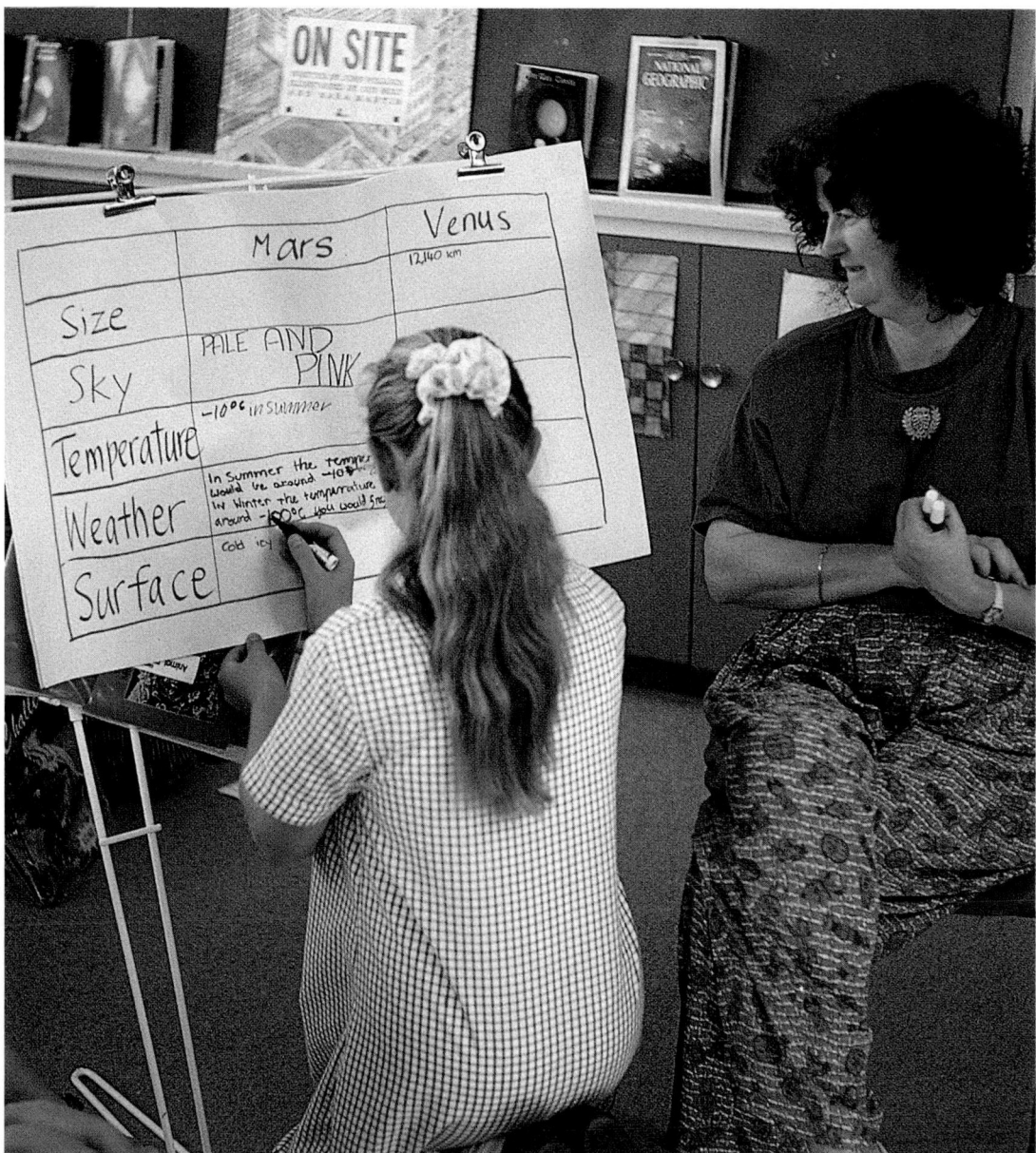

Left. Children brain-storm "answers" to the clues in the big book on the teacher's left. The teacher writes down all their suggestions on the chart on her right.
Below. Children review each other's suggestions before arriving at an agreed prediction.

What's that animal ~~hidden~~ in the grass?
~~...~~ a lizard.

butterfly
~~cicada~~
snake
dragonfly
~~worm~~
earthworm
~~lizard~~
caterpillar
~~toad~~
~~egg~~
walking stick

What is Informazing?

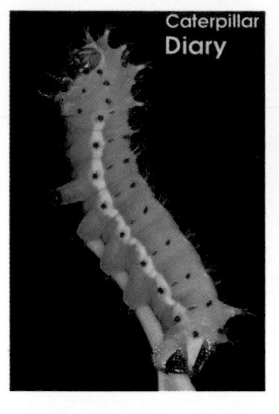

Informazing consists of twenty-two books. Topics covered in the Informazing books include:

- prehistory
- animals
- space
- the body
- physical matter
- conservation

The Informazing titles appeal to the imagination of children and provide interest and learning for all grade levels K-8. However, there are differences in reading level, interest and concepts. Suggested grade levels have been indicated in the overview chart (see pages 12–16 below).

You may at times wish to use a book at a level different from those suggested. For example we have suggested that *Creature Features* is suitable for children from kindergarten to grade 3. But this book has been used successfully in grade 4 to conclude a topic on small creatures, and in grade 6 for introducing classification of animals focusing on their specific features.

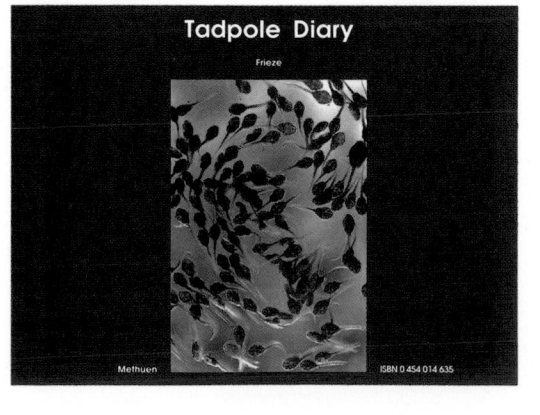

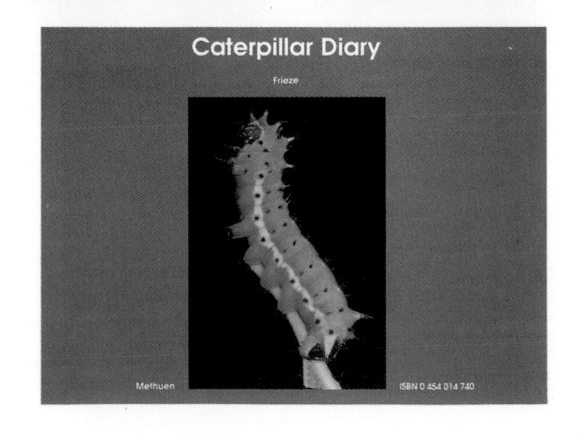

Skeletons

Millions of Years Ago

I Spy

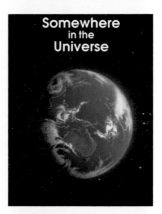

What Did You Eat Today?

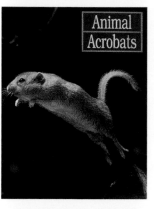

Animal Acrobats

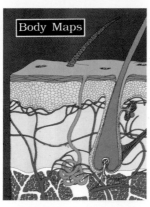

Body Maps

Body Facts

Somewhere in the Universe

Animal, Plant or Mineral?

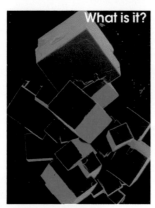

What is it?

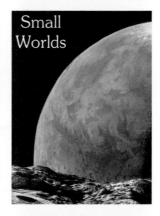

Small Worlds

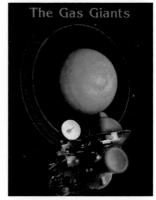

The Gas Giants

The Life of the Butterfly

Frieze

Methuen

ISBN 0 454 014 66X

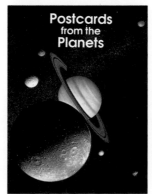

Postcards from the Planets

EARTH in DANGER

Right. Allow children to share their knowledge and experience in pairs or small groups.
Below. Whole-class discussion is just as important as the shared reading of a nonfiction book. The teacher can demonstrate note-taking during the discussion.

Opposite page:

Top. Many *Informazing* books can be used as models for the children's own writing.
Middle. The frieze can be used before, during or after sharing the big book.
Below. Children can label the frieze using removable adhesive note paper.

Children are motivated and excited by both the visual quality of the books and the information they have to offer. Informazing provides a context for a variety of activities which support the development of reading and writing across the curriculum. Children will read for enjoyment, investigate topics of interest, raise questions, and explore issues about the world.

Informazing is available both in big book and in small book format. Friezes (or wallcharts) are available for three of the titles.

Big books

Big books are an essential element of Informazing and can be used in different ways to develop reading, writing and talking. For example:

Reading:

- reading together
- building on predictable text patterns
- examining the conventions of nonfiction books
- introducing vocabulary in context
- developing motivation and confidence which encourages independent reading

Writing:

- demonstrating a variety of forms
- using nonfiction conventions
- transferring information from one text style to another
- writing text using graphic information

Talking:

- sharing information
- contributing prior experience and knowledge
- developing prediction skills
- discussing ideas and issues

The big books provide many opportunities for you to model reading and writing skills as well as to focus on the conventions of nonfiction texts. They provide a shared focus as well as providing a context for research and further learning. The discussion which takes place among the children during a shared reading lesson is as important as the reading itself.

Sharing and rereading the book, allowing the children to interact with one another, summarizing the information and drawing conclusions are all important preparations for writing. Using the big books allows you to involve children in all aspects of language: reading, writing, listening and speaking.

10

Friezes

Friezes (or wallcharts) are available for the three books on the life cycles of the butterfly, the moth and the frog.

The Life of the Butterfly Frieze
Caterpillar Diary Frieze
Tadpole Diary Frieze

There are many strategies for using the friezes, for example:

- Friezes can be used to focus on what is actually happening if live animals are in the classroom.

> In a grade 1 classroom where tadpoles were being studied the teacher moved from the frieze, compared the development of the tadpoles in the aquarium, then went back to the frieze for comparison, and finally wrote up the children's responses.

Such a process acknowledges what children already know and gives them the opportunity to build on and assimilate new knowledge.

- You can cut the frieze into separate pictures, shuffle them, and ask the children to put the frieze into a meaningful sequence. This activity will give the teacher an insight into what the children already know about (for example) tadpoles and frogs.

Such an activity can assist in assessing the prior knowledge of children or their understanding after the book has been shared.

Further uses for the friezes are included with the activities of the relevant books.

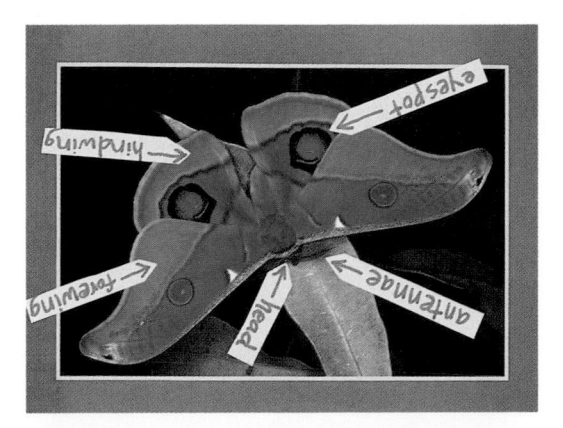

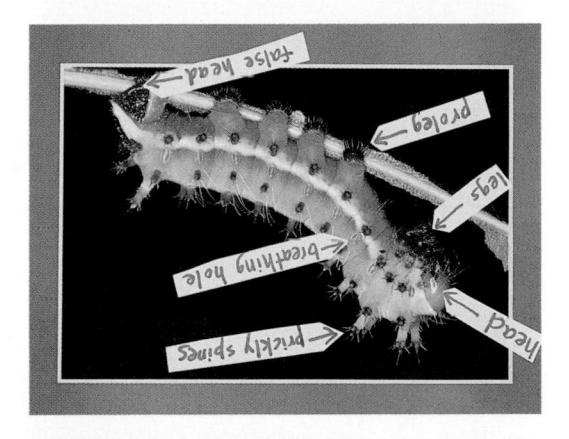

Small books

Many of the suggested activities are intended for pairs or small groups working with the small books.

The small books are used for:

- reading practice:
  - to oneself
  - to others
  - sharing with a partner or a small group
- extracting information
- raising questions
- individual research
- checking references
- solving problems
- taking home to read to parents

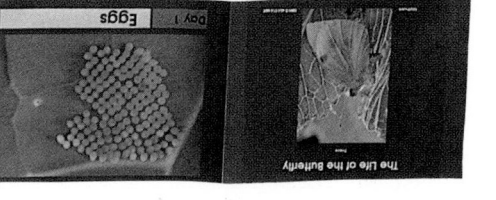

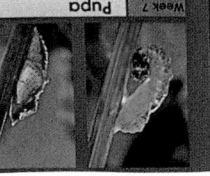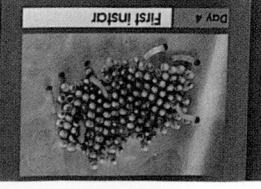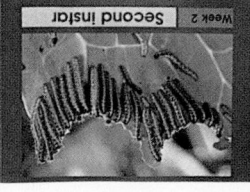

The Life of the Butterfly — Day 1 Eggs · Day 4 First instar · Week 2 Second instar · Week 5 Third instar · Week 7 Pupa

Overview Chart

Book title	Language	Science and Mathematics	Finding and presenting information
Millions of Years Ago Kindergarten–Grade 6 *page 30*	• Writing: –an extended text –a postcard –research findings –information from the pictures –from another point of view	• Concept of a million • Time: –a million years –calendars –time lines • Investigating: –prehistoric animals –extinction	• Compiling: –a contents page –an index • Interpreting diagrams • Using encyclopedias and dictionaries
Mystery Monsters Kindergarten–Grade 4 *page 34*	• Predicting • Writing: –clues –research findings –details of observations –information from pictures • Playing and making games	• Observing and drawing using magnifying glasses • Investigating: –habitats –camouflage –animals • Classifying • Estimating size	• Making picture maps • Using cross references • Extracting information from pictures • Listing
Hidden Animals Kindergarten–Grade 4 *page 38*	• Predicting • Writing: –another text using different animals –research findings as a list	• Investigating: –camouflage –habitats –food chains • Classifying • Observing and drawing animals	• Drawing: –labelled diagrams –picture maps • Compiling: –a glossary –an index • Making a chart • Making a collage: –using photographs –using natural materials
Skeletons Grades 2–8 *page 42*	• Predicting • Writing: –research findings –lists for research • Vocabulary: –scientific names	• Investigating and comparing: –bones –skeletons –specific parts of skeletons • Classifying: –informally –scientifically • Drawing Venn diagrams	• Mapping: –the world • Interpreting: –tables –labelled photographs • Using encyclopedias and dictionaries • Making a table

Book title	Language	Science and Mathematics	Finding and presenting information
Animal Clues Kindergarten–Grade 2 *page 46*	• Predicting • Writing: –clues –information from pictures –a chart –a list for research	• Symmetry • Classifying • Observing and drawing using magnifying glasses	• Compiling an index
Creature Features Kindergarten–Grade 3 *page 50*	• Predicting • Writing: –puzzles –research findings –lists for research • Debating	• Investigating animal features • Observing small creatures using magnifying glasses • Classifying	• Researching: –using books –using pictures • Drawing and labelling pictures • Drawing Venn diagrams
I Spy Kindergarten–Grade 6 *page 54*	• Predicting • Writing: –puzzles –speech bubbles –research findings	• Graphing • Investigating: –eyesight –other body parts –animals • Making a pinhole camera	• Drawing labelled diagrams • Compiling a glossary • Making a poster • Using dictionaries • Making lists
The Book of Animal Records Grades 2–6 *page 58*	• Predicting • Writing: –predictions –other animal records –other records –research findings –a class book	• Creating and solving mathematical problems • Estimating and measuring • Comparing sizes • Recording in different ways • Graphing animals • Classifying	• Making life-size drawings • Studying drawings • Interpreting diagrams • Using: –a contents page –a glossary • Compiling a glossary
What Did You Eat Today? Kindergarten–Grade 6 *page 62*	• Predicting • Writing: –information from a graph to report format –a diary –a letter –puns –about what was learned	• Creating and solving problems • Graphing: –drawing and interpreting pictograms and bar charts • Calendars • Classifying: –food –animals • Animal diets	• Finding graphs • Collecting data on field trips • Listing and presenting information as: –tables –graphs

Overview Chart

Book title	Language	Science and Mathematics	Finding and presenting information
Animal Acrobats Grades 2–6 *page 66*	• Predicting • Writing: –another text –research findings –a report	• Graphing • Time • Length • Scale drawings • Investigating: –camouflage –habitats –features of animals –movement • Classifying	• Using: –a contents page –an index • Comparing a contents page and an index page • Compiling a glossary • Making a chart • Drawing: –predictions –scale diagrams
The Life of the Butterfly Grades 2–6 *page 70*	• Sequencing the frieze • Writing: –predicting the text –a text for the frieze –a class journal –individual diaries –research findings –"mystery facts" –a report • Comparing texts • Vocabulary: –origin of words • Spoken presentation	• Setting up a vivarium • Making scale drawings • Measuring growth • Observing growth and change • Life cycles	• Using and comparing: –a contents page –an index • Using a glossary • Making lists • Compiling: –a glossary –a table of facts • Labelling: –diagrams –the frieze • Using encyclopedias and dictionaries
Caterpillar Diary Kindergarten–Grade 2 *page 74*	• Predicting • Sequencing the frieze • Comparing texts • Writing: –a diary –another text based on a diary –encyclopedia entries –"mystery facts"	• Setting up a vivarium • Observing: –growth and change –using magnifying glasses • Estimating and measuring • Time line • Comparing moths and butterflies	• Drawing and labelling diagrams • Comparing an index and a contents page • Compiling: –a contents page –a table • Making a table • Making life-size or scale drawings • Making a pie chart • Using encyclopedias and dictionaries
Tadpole Diary Kindergarten–Grade 4 *page 78*	• Predicting • Writing: –instructions –a diary –from a different point of view –a text for the frieze –labels for the frieze • Sequencing the frieze • Comparing texts	• Observing: –change and growth –using magnifying glasses –differences • Making life-size drawings • Making scale drawings • Life cycle of a frog • Comparing tadpoles and fish	• Making labelled drawings • Making charts and tables • Comparing diagrams and photographs • Flow charts and pie charts • Compiling: –a glossary –a table

Book title	Language	Science and Mathematics	Finding and presenting information
Body Maps Grades 4–8 *page 82*	• Predicting • Writing –lists –information from diagrams –research findings • Vocabulary: –Greek and Latin roots –origin of words –scientific and everyday terms	• Investigating: –bones and skeletons –x-rays –taste and touch –movement of animals –body parts • Making joints • Observing using magnifying glasses	• Using labelled diagrams and cross sections to: –interpret information –extract information –present information graphically • Using an index • Using color coding • Using dictionaries and encyclopedias • Making lists
Body Facts Grades 4–8 *page 86*	• Predicting • Writing: –predictions –facts –research findings –a chart –a letter –a personal diary –a game	• Investigating large numbers • Investigating: –a number of aspects of the body –living conditions	• Using: –a contents page –an index • Compiling a glossary • Making a chart
Animal, Plant or Mineral? Grades 3–8 *page 90*	• Predicting • Writing: –clues –a class book –research findings • Vocabulary: –origin and meaning of words • Following instructions • Summarizing • Using and discussing question techniques	• Classifying • Observing: –using magnifying glasses and microscopes –drawing using micro-scopes • Investigating materials	• Summarizing information • Drawing items and labelling them • Using encyclopedias and dictionaries • Taking notes
What Is It? Grades 3–8 *page 94*	• Predicting • Writing: –clues –research findings –a diary	• Observing: –using a microscope –and drawing using microscopes; • Investigating use of instruments • Growing crystals	• Researching: –subject headings –cataloguing procedures • Using photographs

Overview Chart

Book title	Language	Science and Mathematics	Finding and presenting information
Somewhere in the Universe Kindergarten–Grade 6 *page 98*	• Predicting • Writing: –letters –addresses on envelopes –research findings –a class book	• Representing the solar system: –with people –with models • Investigating: –the planets –the universe • Observing the night sky • Reading and making maps: –of the world –of school or home • Maps and globes	• Presenting information graphically • Making maps: –of home –of school
Postcards from the Planets Grades 4–8 *page 102*	• Writing: –postcards and letters –dates and addresses –newspaper reports –a diary • Characterization and humor • Fact and fiction	• Making a time line • Investigating: –the planets –space travel • Observing the night sky	• Researching: –subject headings –cataloguing principles • Using encyclopedias and dictionaries • Note taking
Small Worlds **The Gas Giants** Grades 4–8 *page 106*	• Predicting • Writing: –weather forecasts –research findings –notes for illustrations –descriptions –poems	• Making a time line • Investigating: –planets –temperature –evaporation, melting, freezing (gas, liquid, solid) –geology –skies on different planets –the weather on Earth –the weather on other planets –days and years • Predicting size and distance	• Studying: –a variety of graphics –cross sections and maps –labelled diagrams • Using or compiling: –a contents page –a glossary –an index • Using encyclopedias and dictionaries
Earth in Danger Grades 4–8 *page 112*	• Predicting • Writing –a newspaper article –recommendations for action • Debating	• Global warming • Graphs • Making a terrarium • World maps • Climate • Recycling	• Interpreting graphic information • Extracting information from newspapers

Reading and writing nonfiction   *Part 1*

Left. Children write and illustrate their own "creature feature" puzzles modelled on the big book they have read.

Below left. After observing cross section diagrams in *Body Maps* Chris researched other animals and presented his writing in the form of a labelled cross section.

Below right. Nonfiction texts often feature an impersonal tone, generalizations and technical terms.

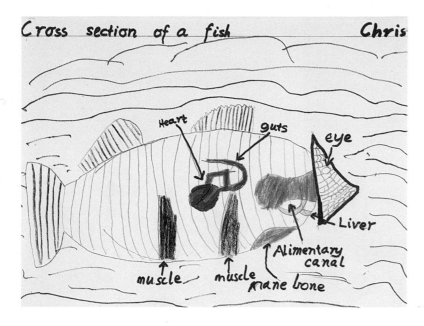

Cross section of a fish   Chris

Heart
guts
eye
Liver
muscle   muscle
mane bone
Alimentary canal

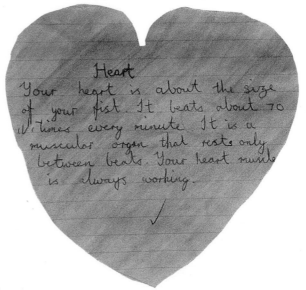

Heart
Your heart is about the size of your fist. It beats about 70 times every minute. It is a muscular organ that rests only between beats. Your heart muscle is always working.

Informazing: Learning and teaching

Children are actively involved

Informazing is presented in ways which actively involve children. But being actively involved is more than simply doing. It also implies thinking, reflecting and having a personal stake in the outcome of an activity. Thus, in writing clues for an animal puzzle modelled on, for example, *Animal Clues*, children will be thinking about the features of the animal and reflecting on these features as clues. Children will have a real purpose for the activity: to make a puzzle to present to another person.

Below. Research is not always done with books. The parts of a skeleton were brought into this grade 5/6 classroom and the children were given the task of interpreting the ways in which the bones interconnect.
Below right. Research can include studying animals in the classroom, discussing observations, comparing experiences and writing these down.

Children learn from direct experiences

Because the Informazing books are of great interest, children will bring to the books their own knowledge and experience, on which new knowledge and understanding can be built. The activities developed for each book provide children with direct experiences: for example, keeping and observing caterpillars, or observing objects under microscopes and magnifying glasses.

Direct experiences are fundamental to the development of learning with understanding. It is the interaction between

- the children's prior knowledge,
- their direct experience,
- book learning,
- discussion and
- the reflection on all of these

which makes for effective learning.

Children learn from each other

The variety of activities offered in the Informazing books provides children with many opportunities to learn from each other. For example:

- listening to each other during a shared reading;
- writing clues in pairs;
- extracting information from the small books in a small group;
- researching information together;
- making models.

Children make connections across subject areas

The curriculum should be viewed as a whole and not as a collection of small areas of learning. Informazing gives you opportunities to be involved in a number of subject areas while exploring one topic. For example when using *Postcards from the Planets* you and the children can be involved in many activities:

- reading
- writing fiction
- writing nonfiction
- extracting information
- mathematics
- learning about astronomy
- looking at space technology
- discussing newspaper reporting
- debating issues
- letter writing

The interaction with this one text and the associated activities encourages children to make meaningful connections between all these areas of learning. You may need to make the links explicit, and give children opportunities to reflect on the connections.

Children are able to experiment

Experimenting with different forms of writing, proposing different points of view, asking questions such as "What if . . .?" and solving problems are all important to learning.

Trying out new ideas and experimenting can occur in a number of ways; teachers need to model these strategies and to give children the opportunity to try them out. For example:

- writing in different forms;
- presenting information in different ways;
- debating issues from different points of view;
- asking questions such as "What if . . .;"
- testing ideas through discussion, observation, and experimentation.

Conclusion

A classroom in which reading and writing are valued and in which children meet the challenge of discovering and understanding the world with enthusiasm is a positive learning environment. You can help to provide such an environment by demonstrating the strategies children need to learn as well as demonstrating your own enjoyment and interest in learning. You can also support children by valuing their contributions, and by challenging them to develop further their skills, their thinking, and their interests.

Above. Reading and counting the animal parts in *Creature Features* can lead to mathematics activities.
Left. To make their own *Creature Feature* puzzles children demonstrate language, crafts, and mathematics strategies.
Below. In small groups children can observe, share knowledge, raise questions for investigation, and take notes.

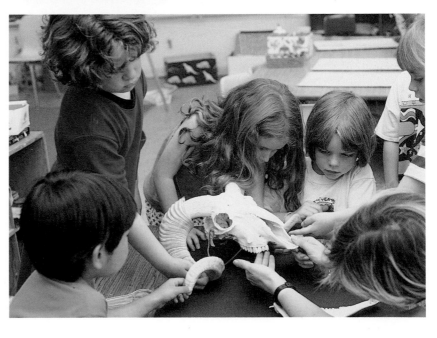

19

Reading, writing and talking across the curriculum

Reading

When reading an Informazing book, you and the children need time to discuss the information and ideas in the book. Be prepared for incidental discussion which is an important part of the "reading." This shared experience becomes the basis for the development of reading, writing, thinking and research skills.

Some texts are particularly suitable for supporting children's reading development. For example, *Animal Clues* and *Hidden Animals* have repetitive structures which support children but allow them to contribute their own knowledge and experience. However, these books are also valuable for research and investigations by older children.

In developing reading skills with the big books, a number of strategies can be used.

Children can:

- direct the shared reading which gives the children confidence as readers and provides valuable reading practice;
- predict the pattern of the text: this assists younger children in their reading, and provides a model for older children's writing;
- be involved in scanning the text, and in finding specific information;
- demonstrate the use of an index, contents page or glossary.

Teachers can:

- focus on nonfiction writing conventions within the text: headings, captions, cross references, tables, lists, etc.;
- discuss the variety of purposes for writing and the forms that suit these purposes;
- discuss the styles of language used in different forms of writing;
- demonstrate the use of an index, contents page and glossary;
- discuss and interpret graphic information such as labelled diagrams, graphs, cross sections, maps, time lines, etc.;
- introduce and discuss new vocabulary;
- discuss the meaning, spelling and origin of words, for example the Greek and Latin roots of many scientific and technical terms;
- focus on aspects of punctuation: capital letters, question marks, etc.

All these skills can be further developed and consolidated as children read the small books, independently or in small groups. Skimming can be developed as children use their focus questions for finding information. Children can share the books with their families, which provides further reading practice.

Writing

Informazing provides models and stimulus for writing across most curriculum areas. Children are given opportunities to be involved in factual writing and at the same time to use their imagination.

Children need to develop an understanding of the subtle differences which exist in the many writing styles and texts they experience. Informazing assists children to use scientific, instructional and reporting texts as well as descriptive or narrative texts.

Taking research information in one form (such as a map) and presenting it in another form (such as a table) gives children opportunities to manipulate language. Children can take notes of an experiment and transfer the writing into a report, or extract facts from a report to make a table. Such activities give you insight into the children's understanding of the material, and can provide valuable assessment opportunities.

These suggestions are not exhaustive and both teachers and children should experiment with other techniques. For instance:

Transferring information into another style or form

- *Visual information can be presented as text.* Children can write descriptions of the animals in *Animal Clues* using the visual information provided in the photographs.

- *Graphic information can be presented as text, in a variety of styles.* Children can take a graph from *What Did You Eat Today?* and write instructions to the zoo keeper responsible for feeding the animal.

- *Text can be presented in a variety of graphic forms.* Children can make a graph to show the food eaten by a butterfly at different stages of its life cycle using the tables in *The Life of the Butterfly.* After reading *The Gas Giants* or *Small Worlds* children can extract

Opposite page.

Top. *Informazing* big books are good for reading alone.
Middle. After reading *Mystery Monsters* David summarized the book's information in the form of a map.
Bottom. When a dragonfly was brought to school the children were encouraged to share their knowledge about small animals. This led to an "I Spy" text about dragonflies (illustrated on page 29 below).

information from the text to make a diagram with labels about a particular planet.

Presenting new information in another style or form

Informazing provides children with experience in interpreting and using a variety of ways to present information. Children can experiment with styles and forms. For example:

● After reading *Postcards from the Planets* and *Body Maps*, children can research other body systems and write postcards from different parts of the body.

● Children can use color coding to show the bones of animals' back legs after studying the diagrams of front legs on pages 4 and 5 of *Body Maps*.

● Children can make up their information puzzles using the format of *Animal, Plant or Mineral?*

● After playing the board game in *Mystery Monsters*, children can create a board game for the animals in *The Book of Animal Records* or for other items they have researched.

Working with nonfiction conventions

● Children can make contents pages, indexes and glossaries, using the models given in other Informazing books.

● Headings, subheadings and captions for children's own work can be modelled on those in the Informazing books.

● Note-taking skills can be developed, for instance in listing the factual information given in *Postcards from the Planets*.

Talking

Taking time to talk using the big books

When sharing the big books there are a number of ways in which the children's talk can contribute to the topic under investigation. By demonstrating that such talk is valued you are supporting children's literacy development.

Children are given the opportunity to contribute their own experience and knowledge

Informazing contains topics which are of high interest to children. Children can contribute

their prior knowledge and experience of these areas in the classroom. For example, when reading *Animal Clues* children will contribute information and their own experience of the animals in the book. When exploring *The Gas Giants* children will offer their own knowledge about the planets. Such information is valuable when further ideas are discussed and when children move on to a writing or research task.

Children are given the opportunity to discuss their ideas

When the ideas in a book are under discussion children will bring together their direct experience and their knowledge from newspapers, television, field trips and other sources. An example of this is in *Earth in Danger* where topical issues (such as the greenhouse effect) will be familiar to children. The game books such as *Mystery Monsters* and *Animal, Plant or Mineral?* will give children ample opportunity to contribute their own experience. They can use their knowledge to make guesses, and assess suggestions.

> "It could be part of a fish, because they could be scales."

> "It can't be a spider because it has ten legs, and spiders have eight."

This provides a context for the children to assimilate the ideas into their own knowledge and experience, and to extend their knowledge.

Children are given the opportunity to listen to others' ideas

When groups of children make their own investigations and report their findings to the class, there is often great interest in listening to their findings. Because the children have been involved in a variety of aspects within the topic, new information is being presented, often in a variety of ways, and children are not just listening to the same information being presented over and over again.

Informazing offers a number of opportunities for solving problems. In the puzzle and game books the information is given to the children in pieces. In trying to solve the puzzle the children build on each other's comments and suggestions. To do this successfully it is necessary that they listen to each other and assess each other's contributions.

Children talking about their work

Reading, writing and research skills will develop more fully in a context where ideas are explored and processes modelled in discussion. Talk should precede writing and should continue throughout any unit of work. Children should be encouraged to discuss their presentations and to give constructive criticism to others.

In order to learn how to do this the teacher needs to model some alternative ways. Some children will need time and support to develop both the confidence and the skills necessary to participate in some of the ideas set out below. Children need not always report to the whole class; you can ask pairs and small groups to report to one another and you can move among the groups, observing and assessing their performance.

There are a number of ways in which children can present information orally. Those which follow each have a different focus.

Before beginning research

Before research is undertaken the children can tell the class what they intend to do. For example, "These are the questions we are going to find out about." "We have decided to focus on this part of the issue." All the books lend themselves to this approach.

After completing an investigation

After the research is completed, the information children have prepared can be presented formally. The material may be a table, a drawing, an illustration, or a labelled diagram, which the children explain to the class. Research need not always be presented in the form of a written text.

Presenting drafts for response

Children can present their work orally in draft form for response from others before the final copies are made or written. Many books, and in particular the game and puzzle books, lend themselves to this approach. By assessing the response of others, children can reassess their methods and information, and refine their presentation.

> In presenting their drafts for *What Is It?*, one pair of children from a grade 6 class used the clue "they are bears" for "pandas." They were challenged by another child who said that pandas were not bears. This meant that they had to research and check their information.

After completing writing

When the writing task is completed children can share their final copies with others, reading aloud and discussing the process from the beginning of the writing to the final copy.

Debating issues

Older children will enjoy debating issues such as the "greenhouse effect," animals in danger, or why dinosaurs died out. Asking children to talk to both sides of the argument or the side they disagree with makes them see the other point of view and also assists them to construct arguments.

Imaginative presentations

Children can present the work imaginatively. For example, they can use the frieze for an oral presentation of *The Life of the Butterfly* or give a dramatic presentation of *Postcards from the Planets*.

Lists and notes

Children can present notes of information or lists of groupings or classifications, at different stages in the activity or within the topic, justifying and giving reasons for their decisions. This is particularly effective when children are involved in a classification activity and the classifications from each group are different.

The science program

The Informazing books deal with scientific topics, but they do not "teach" science. For children to understand concepts it is essential that they are involved in scientific activities, such as investigating, observing, experimenting, classifying, discussing, writing, and reflecting.

Informazing provides many opportunities for these kinds of activities, as well as providing information which can be integrated with their own observations and experiments to develop their understanding of natural phenomena. The activities suggested for individual Informazing books will assist in providing the link between the information and the children's understanding.

Observing

Accurate observation is developed through activities such as:

- outdoor searches for particular items;
- using magnifying glasses;
- drawing directly from life, and drawing what can be seen under a magnifying glass or microscope;
- labelling drawings;
- discussing differences and similarities;
- presenting oral or written descriptions of observations.

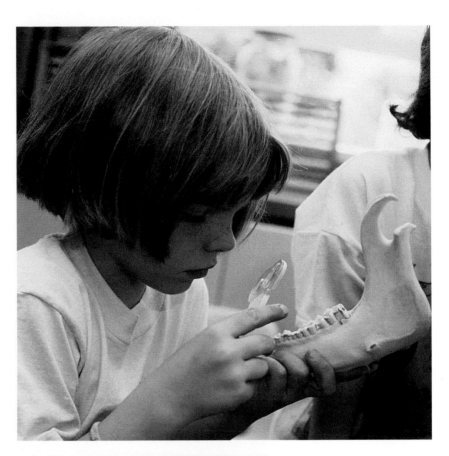

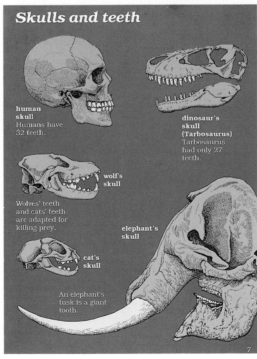

Skulls and teeth

human skull
Humans have 32 teeth.

dinosaur's skull (Tarbosaurus)
Tarbosaurus had only 27 teeth.

wolf's skull

Wolves' teeth and cats' teeth are adapted for killing prey.

elephant's skull

cat's skull

An elephant's tusk is a giant tooth.

7

Allow children to write and draw what they can observe (**above**) before you present the text to them (**left**). This helps you and the children to focus the purpose of the reading.

The Informazing books provide models to assist children in making and recording observations, through the detailed photographs, labelled diagrams, color-coded diagrams, cross sections, and so on.

Experimenting

The statements made in the Informazing books should not be accepted uncritically, but wherever possible should be verified by observation or experimentation. For example:

- Children can experiment with taste on the different parts of their tongue after reading *Body Maps*.

- After reading *What Is It?* children may not be able to observe a fly's eye under a microscope, but it should be possible to observe a drop of water, a hair, Velcro, or salt under a magnifying lens, and to compare these with other objects.

- It is not possible to verify that the human eye "sees" an inverted image (as discussed in *I Spy*), but the principle can be shown by making a pinhole camera.

The activities suggested in this book do not "prove" the truth of statements in the Informazing books, but do serve to explain them in terms which children can understand and assimilate.

Classifying

Classification skills are important because classification is basic to the way in which we organize knowledge and make sense of the world. Children need opportunities to classify items in their own ways and for meaningful purposes before they are ready to use and understand conventional scientific classification schemes.

When children classify or group items, they should be challenged to justify their groupings, and to discuss the ways in which the classification can be useful. For example, to classify foods as ones they like or don't like will be of use in planning a birthday party, but only of limited use in planning a healthy and balanced diet. To find out more information about an animal, it may be more useful to classify it as a mammal, bird, or reptile than as a zoo animal or a farm animal.

Information from a classification activity can often be used as a starting point for a different activity.

Mathematics: measuring, calculating and comparing

Understanding and operating with mathematical concepts is important in understanding most of the topics in these books. Informazing provides many opportunities for using mathematics in context, for example:

- estimating
- investigating time
- simple counting and matching
- measuring and comparing length
- measuring and comparing weight
- comparing distances
- using scale drawings
- drawing maps
- measuring and comparing temperature
- solving problems

Besides providing opportunities for children to use mathematics in meaningful contexts, Informazing also provides the stimulus for investigating mathematical concepts.

Arts and crafts

Children will naturally be involved in many arts and crafts experiences as they move through the suggested activities. For example, they will be drawing, painting, constructing, and making collages. You may also wish to focus on specific techniques as the opportunities arise.

Many examples of children's artwork are included in the illustrations in this book: the accompanying captions suggest appropriate arts and crafts activities.

Problem solving, puzzles and games

Eight Informazing books are presented as puzzles (based on familiar games, as in *I Spy* and *Animal Plant or Mineral?*, or on visual information as in *Animal Clues*, or on particular features of animals as in *Skeletons*). Through the process of solving, discussing, and making up puzzles, children develop logical thinking skills, by:

- predicting
- observing
- describing
- discriminating
- classifying
- listening
- assessing
- eliminating
- justifying

Reading the book and solving the puzzles

As the book is shared, children predict the solutions, assess each other's contributions, eliminate some possibilities and justify their responses. The children's responses should be written up on the chalkboard or a large sheet of paper, to be referred to as the book is shared.

The puzzle element is appealing, the subject matter interests the children, and they are being given the opportunity to contribute their own knowledge and experience and to use their imagination. Children are genuinely interested in listening to other children's work. Interaction between the children is extremely important and valuable. The children should defend their guesses based on the accumulation of information.

Your role is to ensure that children have the opportunity to express their ideas. There is also a need to stop and ask the children to summarize the information at appropriate points in the discussion. This not only gives them thinking time but also models the way in which information can be summarized.

Some of the books can be introduced by playing the game *before* sharing the book, as suggested for *I Spy* and *Animal, Plant or Mineral?* This assists children to think more clearly about the information given in each of the clues when the book is read.

> *Animal, Plant or Mineral?* was presented to two grade 6 classes. One class played the game first and the other class immediately read the book. The children who had played the game first thought more about the information given in each of the clues when it came to reading the book. These children also summarized their information and thought more carefully about their next questions.

Reflection on and discussion of the clues is important before children move on to constructing their own puzzles. This discussion can focus on:

- What information helped?
- How did the picture help?
- What helped us to eliminate some guesses?
- Which clues were really difficult?
- Which clues were too easy?

Children can reread these books frequently with each other after the shared reading. They can also read the books to their families, and to children in other classes.

Making up puzzles

After sharing the books, children can make up their own puzzles. They need to discuss

Above. *What Did You Eat Today?* leads naturally to counting and matching activities in mathematics.
Left. In making their own "mystery monsters" children combine language with arts and crafts.
Below. Ask children to justify their predictions with reference to both the picture and the text.

and sift information in order to write appropriate clues.

Opportunities are provided for children to manipulate language. If a descriptive text is taken and transformed into clues, children need to fully comprehend the text they are reading. Such an activity gives the teacher insight into children's comprehension of the material.

Presenting their puzzles orally before finalizing their written form is an important stage which assists the children in refining their puzzles.

A grade 6 class presented the clues orally for *What Is It?* This assisted the children when they came to the writing task. There were opportunities to discuss the difference between purely descriptive language and language which offers additional useful information. Some children's presentations were challenged, which highlighted the need for further research.

Research

Informazing provides a strong context for investigation and encourages children to be involved in research activities. Children can move from the context of the book to doing research. They will return to the books for a variety of reasons. For example:

- to clarify their research focus;
- to find different ways to present their information;
- to check information;
- to read for pleasure;
- to compare information from other sources.

Constructing questions

Before children consult other reference books, they need to identify a focus. An effective way of doing this is by constructing questions.

- This can be done before reading the book as suggested on page 70 below for *The Life of the Butterfly* where children compiled a chart of "what we know" and "what we want to find out."
- When sharing the big book, children's questions can be listed on a wallchart as they arise, and can form the basis of research later.
- Children can study the small books, in pairs or small groups, decide what they want to find out and then construct questions.

Sources of information

When children are involved in carrying out research activities, they need to discuss the method of finding the information as well as to decide what information is important. Before they move to the class library or school library, they should list the ways in which they will try to find the information:

- Do they know a particular book they might use?
- Are there resources other than books which can be used?
- Will they use an encyclopedia or an atlas?
- Will they use the library catalogue?
- What entries will they try first?
- If they are unsuccessful with the first book or entry they look up, what other strategies can they use?

All information may not be available in the school library, and the children should be encouraged to seek information from other places, for example by telephoning local museums, laboratories, universities, or libraries. A list of these contacts can be built up for use throughout the year. The children should be made aware that information does not only come in books: for example, it also comes in posters, video and audio tapes, microfiches, computer programs, etc.

"Is that really true?"

This is a popular question from children, which may be provoked by reading books such as *Postcards from the Planets* or *Body Facts*.

Facts are not forever. There can be changes in phenomena, natural, social or political. Volcanoes and earthquakes can change the landscape, countries can change their names or their governments, laws can change, and populations can alter.

There can also be changes in our knowledge and understanding of phenomena, and new information can supplement or contradict former beliefs. Six new moons and five rings around Neptune were discovered in 1989 while one of the books in this series was about to go to press (*The Gas Giants*, page 9). Predictions about the "greenhouse effect" were revised in 1990 during the writing of *Earth in Danger*.

Some books offer information in a fictional form, and children need to understand which parts are fact and which are imagined narrative. *Postcards from the Planets* is a striking example of a text that conveys information through narrative.

Involving families

Informazing provides a number of ways in which you can involve families in their children's learning. This family involvement reinforces the work which is being done at school while giving the family the opportunity to share in what their children are doing at school.

At home families can:

- read the small books with their children;
- play the learning games from the books with their children;
- read the books and play the games which children have made at school.

Other activities include:

- observing a pet;
- observing the night sky;
- talking about what things are made of;
- researching information;
- discussing things when on outings, for example, at the park, or the zoo, or driving in the car.

At school families can:

- be invited to view displays or performances;
- read with a small group;
- write with a small group;
- contribute special skills or knowledge, for example, professional skills, experience with animals, special hobbies or interests;
- be invited to join the children on field trips.

Such an approach increases the confidence of parents as educators of their children as well as enriching their experiences with them.

Classroom organization
Access to books

You and your school will need to make decisions about the storage of and access to the Informazing books. For many of the activities, it will be helpful to have copies of other Informazing books available in your classroom, for example:

- to extend information on a topic;
- to provide examples of nonfiction conventions;
- to provide examples of alternative ways of presenting information;
- to model skimming and finding information, and using features such as indexes and glossaries.

Evaluation

When developing and working with a topic, you need to keep in mind the purposes for the individual activities which you present to children. The focus within a unit of work may move from developing knowledge of a particular area of content to developing specific reading, writing, and recording skills in nonfiction.

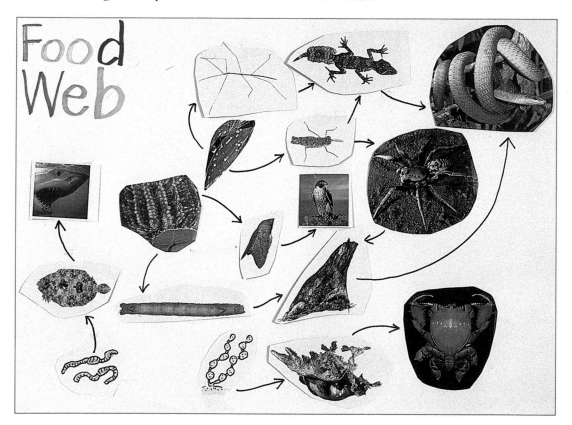

Left. A food web diagram can be used to summarize the information in *Hidden Animals*. Children can also add other animals to the web.

In evaluation, it is necessary to keep the objectives of the unit or activity strongly in mind, while being aware of and responsive to the skills or concepts which children address as they work through an activity.

For example, if an index is being made for *Animal Clues,* many skills may be addressed simultaneously:

- reading other indexes
- using an index
- putting words in alphabetical order
- finding out the meanings of new words
- selecting relevant information
- developing the ability to summarize information efficiently.

While the major focus for a particular group of children may be the selection of the words for the index, the activity may also provide you with information on some of the other skills which children are using.

Evaluating oral language

Using the big books to introduce topics and predict texts gives you plenty of opportunities to observe the children's oral language. In this role you should encourage discussion among the children, which you can evaluate. Small group discussions, working in pairs and small groups, and the presentation of information to others are occasions when you can observe and note children's participation and development.

Observing children

As a skilled observer you have the responsibility of recording significant information in a busy classroom. In order to make sense out of all the activity taking place in a classroom, you will need to focus on a particular aspect of learning, and on one child or a small group of children. At the same time, you will need to be flexible enough to note other events which may be important. A short space of time at the end of the session or the day is often sufficient for reflection on classroom happenings. The use of a class list here is invaluable.

You cannot of course record all the events of the day, but you may decide to note a particular aspect for all children, for example whether they can put words in alphabetical order. Beyond this, significant moments only need to be recorded on the class list, for example, when a child demonstrates a skill that you did not expect from that individual, or, conversely, when a child shows a lack of understanding which you had expected to observe.

Work samples

The writing and recording from the activities provide a wealth of material for evaluation of the program as well as for the assessment of individual children. Keep samples which provide evidence of different skills as well as samples which focus on the particular topic being investigated. Examples of children's work can include charts, tables, graphs, and other alternatives for presenting information.

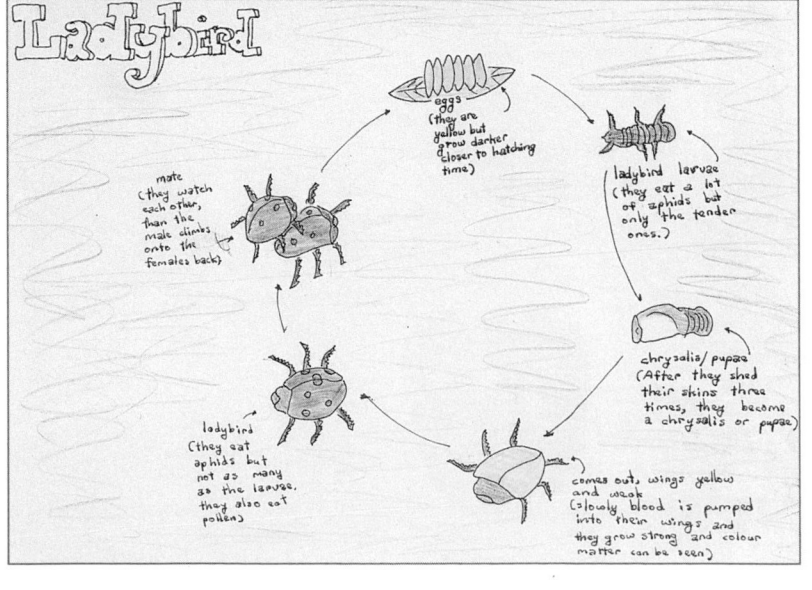

Working with Informazing *Part 2*

This part of *The Informazing Resource Book* suggests classroom activities to accompany each of the twenty-two titles in the Informazing series. The books have been arranged in clusters according to their topic content.

You can select from these activities the ones which are more appropriate for your class. Remember the books can be revisited for different purposes and topics. For example, *What Did You Eat Today?* is useful for a nutrition topic, but is also suitable to be used in mathematics or as preparation for a visit to the zoo.

"Text features" and "graphic features"

At the beginning of the activities for each book there is a list of the *text features* and the *graphic features* of the book. You can consult these if you wish to model specific nonfiction conventions.

"You may need"

A list of the materials which may be needed is provided for each book under the heading *You may need.* You can decide which activities you intend to select before collecting the appropriate materials. It is assumed that paper, pencils, felt pens and other writing and drawing materials will be readily accessible to the children.

Worksheets for photocopying

Worksheets are included at the back of this book (pages 117–133).

"Links with other Informazing books"

This section is designed to assist you to find other references within the Informazing series as you work on a particular book. For example, when looking at the magnified picture of hair on page 6 of *What Is It?*, children may wish to find out more about hair by consulting *Body Maps*, pages 10 and 11, *Body Facts* page 11 or *Animal, Plant or Mineral?* page 7.

By referring to this section, teachers can:

- maximize the use of the Informazing books;
- model the use of cross references;
- demonstrate different ways of looking at or presenting information.

Millions of Years Ago

A journey through time starting 3,500 million years ago when life on Earth began.

Features of the book

Text style	Graphic features
• Report language	• Cross sections
	• Time line
Text features	• Chart using silhouettes (pp. 16–17)
• Additional information in margin of big book	• Color coding
	• Labelled illustrations

Above. Introduce the concept of time starting with the children's own life histories.
Right. Annie's diagram emphasizes that in the age of dinosaurs there were "no [people] in there."
Below right. Some diagrams summarize information, such as this interpretation of the illustration on page 31 opposite. The child's drawing shows the animals from a different perspective in order to compare their relative sizes.

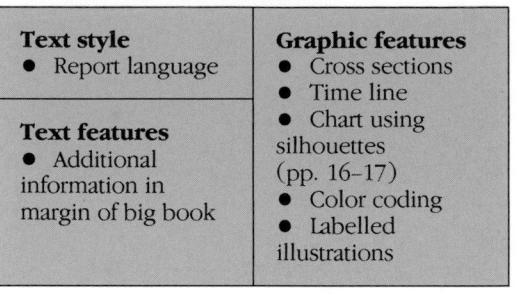

You may need

- big book
- small books
- large sheets of paper
- paints

Introducing the book

What is a million?

- Show the book cover and title. Ask the question: *what is a million?*

- Older students can find a million of something in the school and present the information. (Some examples: grains of sand in the bricks, or pores in the leaves of trees on the school grounds. Children first estimate how many are in each leaf or brick, and then estimate the number of leaves or bricks.)

> **Compare texts:** *Body Facts*, *The Gas Giants* and *Small Worlds* are excellent sources for discussing large numbers.

What is a million years?

- The children could do some calendar work to try and understand such an expanse of time. If a hundred-year calendar is available the children could count the number of months and days and compare this with a twelve-month calendar or even a five-year diary.

- Consult *The Guinness Book of Records* to find the creature that can live the longest, and the creature which lives for the shortest period.

- Individually the children can make time lines of their own life. Give them separate pieces of cardboard on which to record chosen events. These can be hung across the classroom and read by others.

- Ask the children to find out how many years ago their parents were born, and to do the same for their grandparents. From this information, establish that a generation is approximately thirty years.

- Older children will be able to calculate the number of generations to a million years. How many "greats" will they need to add to "grandparents" for their ancestors of a million years ago?

> **Teaching hint:** By first focusing on the significant events that have taken place in the children's own lifetime of about ten years, and then on the number of generations in a million years, children will gain some appreciation of the time scale involved.

Sharing the book

- Read the book through with the children, giving them time to comment on and respond to the pictures. On the first reading, ignore the "Picture Talk" in the margin of the big book unless questions are raised which make it appropriate to consult the information.

> The children knew that dinosaurs were going to appear in this book. They greeted them with great excitement when they first appeared. Lots of discussion took place about the dinosaurs and in particular the reasons why they became extinct.
> —*Grade 6 teacher*
>
> The children spent quite a time discussing each picture. The pages were turned back and forth continually to compare how the Earth was developing.
> —*Grade 6 teacher*
>
> Children in their first year at school were fascinated by the development of the Earth and were as enthusiastic as the older children about the dinosaurs.
> —*Kindergarten teacher*

On subsequent readings, involve the children in more of the book's print features, such as the time line and the "Picture Talk."

"Take a prehistoric walk"

- The time line concept can be more fully understood by an activity such as "Take a prehistoric walk" (see page 16 of the big book *Millions of Years Ago*).

> The children's personal physical involvement in this activity helps them to relate the concept to their own direct experience, and also improves long-term recall of knowledge and skills.

Writing

Extending the text

- Using the small books individual children or small groups of children read the book together and then write an extended text by using the pictures as the source of information. (See also "Changes to the land," page 33 below.)

A day in the life of . . .

- Each child can choose a page of the book and an animal which appears on the page. Write a description of a day from the viewpoint of that animal. Before children start writing, discuss some of the aspects they might include, for example:

  - what do I see?
  - what do I eat?
  - where do I live?
  - will another creature try to eat me?

The "Picture Talk" in the big book *Millions of Years Ago* is a useful resource for this activity.

Below. The age of amphibians (pages 10-11). Compare this illustration with the child's pictorial summary of it on page 30 opposite.

giant dragonfly

horsetails

walking fish

giant amphibian

tree ferns

hammerhead amphibian

giant millipede

spider

Prehistory 31

Children can develop their own texts from careful observation of the pictures in *Millions of Years Ago.* Further research using other reference books may be needed to check the accuracy of these interpretations.

Millions of years ago the world was dark. There were lots of clouds. There were storms with thunder and lightening. The water crashed on the rocks. The volcanoes were errupting.

THE AGE OF REPTILES

200 million years ago vegetation was thick and dense.

Trees were taller and there was a variety of plants.

land was starting to be a life support for reptiles and some dinosours.

The land wasn't so barren and the volcanoes had subsided and become less active.

Postcards from the past

● Imagine that you are a time traveller, and have arrived in one of the prehistoric ages of this book. Send a postcard home, telling your impressions of this age.

> **Compare texts:** *Postcards from the Planets* depicts a journey around the planets through postcards sent back to Earth reporting on the journey. This book can be used as a model for the children's "postcards from the past."

Research

Constructing questions

● In pairs using the small books the children choose a page and list three things they wish to find out about a specific age. For example:

Age of Reptiles:

● What is it that makes an animal a reptile?

● What kind of climate do reptiles need to survive?

● What reptiles on the page are now extinct?

Finding answers

● Some of the children's questions will be answered by the "Picture Talk." For others, children will need to consult other reference books.

Investigating prehistoric animals

● Using this book and other references, the children build up a list of animals arranged by prehistoric period. Collate the information to make a class chart.

● On a museum visit, children can focus on prehistoric animals. Ask them to look for details such as teeth, claws, skin coverings, crests, fins, wings, etc.

> A *Book of Extinct Animal Records* could be made, using *The Book of Animal Records* as a model.

Animals in danger

● Discuss some of the theories about why animals become extinct. Some children are likely to be aware of theories such as a change of climate or the destruction of the environment caused by meteors.

● Point out that extinction is still happening today. Ask children if they know of any animals which have become extinct in more recent times, or are in danger now.

● Discuss what causes animals to become extinct or endangered. Reasons could include hunting by humans, destruction of habitat, lack of food, and chemicals such as pesticides.

● Working in pairs or small groups, the children can find out about an animal which is in danger of extinction. They can use the worksheet "I'm in Danger" (page 119 below) as a framework.

> *Earth in Danger* explores further reasons for extinction.

● Older children, after researching the issues involved in the extinction of animals, can debate these.

Changes to the land

● Read the book again examining the formation and development of the land and the sea. Note that on pages 2–9 the picture is clearly divided into two parts: the top half shows the land and the bottom half shows the sea.

● On pages 2–3, discuss the ways in which volcanoes, storms, and waterfalls change the landscape.

● On succeeding pages, point out the appearance and evolution of land vegetation.

● Working in pairs the children can write a text describing the development of the land and sea masses. Their texts could be attached with removable adhesive tape or paper clips to the appropriate pages of the big book, or illustrated to make a class frieze with a time-line displayed beneath.

Book conventions

Contents page

● Younger children can write a contents page for the book.

Index

● Older children can write an index for the book. Give each small group a number of blank cards and ask them to write *one* word and *the page number* on each card.

● The children then sort the cards into alphabetical order to make an index. Some cards may need more than one page number, and the teacher and children should discuss why (the same topic appears on more than one page).

> This use of cards avoids a confusion of words out of order when drafting an index. The cards can be used again for further sorting activities.

Links with other Informazing books

pages 2–3	origin of life on Earth	*The Gas Giants*, p. 16 (origin of the planets)
page 9	fish	*The Book of Animal Records*, p. 13 *Hidden Animals*, pp. 14–15
page 12	reptiles	*The Book of Animal Records*, pp. 10–12

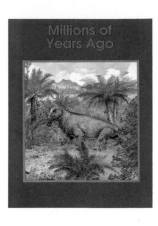

Millions of Years Ago

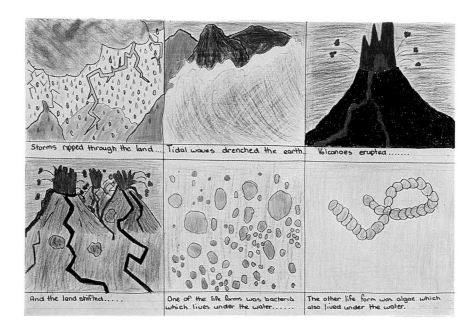

Storms ripped through the land... Tidal waves drenched the earth. Volcanoes erupted.......

And the land shifted..... One of the life forms was bacteria which lives under the water...... The other life form was algae which also lived under the water.

Left. Historical sequences can be built up using a storyboard format.

Prehistory 33

Animal puzzles

Eight of the twenty-two Informazing books are written as puzzles or games. As a learning strategy, the solving of the puzzles immediately engages the children. It stimulates them to think critically about the information presented, to sift and sort the information and to bring their own knowledge to the task. The puzzle format also provides a valuable model for writing.

The three books treated in this chapter focus on animals: *Mystery Monsters* on small creatures, *Hidden Animals* on camouflage, and *Skeletons* on animal skeletons.

Mystery Monsters

A game which involves children in closely observing small creatures.

Features of the book

Text style	Graphic features
● Problem-solving format	● Board game (back cover)
	● Simple color coding:
Text features	–headings
● Instructions	–captions
● Cross references	● High magnification photographs
● Questions and answers	● Other photographs

You may need

- big book
- small books
- pictures of animals from magazines and pamphlets

Before reading the book

● Bring some magnifying glasses into the classroom. Let the children discover that although things look larger through the lens they really remain the same size.

Sharing the book (younger children)

● When using this book with younger children in kindergarten and grade 1, do not attempt to read the entire book at the first session.

● Read two pages at a time inviting the children to discuss them.

● Ask the children to work in pairs recording all the information they know about the particular creatures. When the reading of the book is finished the information can be collated into a chart which shows what the children know. This can be used as a springboard for research.

Sharing the book (older children)

Predicting

Teaching hint: Do not reveal the solutions (pages 14–16) until the whole book has been read, since the children will see the answers to the other mysteries.

● Show the children the front cover, and ask them what they think the monster is. List their responses.

● Read the section "How to use this book" on page 3. Ask the children if they wish to eliminate some of their guesses or make new predictions. Record any changes.

After reading the blurb, a group of grade 3 children eliminated some guesses and added others:

sea anemone	
caterpillar	crab
spitfire	alien
ugly monster	Martian
outer space monster	space slug
extraterrestrial	slug
germ	hairy monster
monster with 300 legs	witchetty grub
	insect

● Remind the children of the experimenting they did with magnifying glasses. Can they say what is happening in the book?

Reading together

Teaching hint: Read the heading on each page; each heading is an additional clue. During the reading, and after each answer is revealed, children should have the opportunity to contribute their knowledge and experience.

● Read through the book, revealing the clues one at a time. Give the children the opportunity to guess as each clue is revealed. List their predictions on a large sheet of paper that all the children can see.

Teaching hint: By listing the children's predictions on a large sheet of paper that all the children can see, their awareness of note-taking is heightened: this is an important aspect of non-fiction reading.

● Encourage the children to assess the suggestions made, and eliminate some of the predictions as they gain more information.

- When all the puzzles and their solutions have been read, turn to pages 14–16 to see photographs of the "whole" creatures.

Collaborative reading

- If you share the big book with only half the class, let each of those who know the answers have a copy of the small book to read with a friend who did not participate in the shared reading. This will give the children additional reading practice with a purpose, and provide positive reinforcement as they demonstrate the book to each other.

> This strategy can be used successfully with other books such as *What Is It?*, *Animal, Plant or Mineral?* or *Skeletons*.

- Give the children time to read the small books in pairs or small groups, so that they become familiar with the information and the ways in which it is presented. Ask them to discuss:
  - the clues which made it difficult for the reader;
  - the clues which made the animal obvious;
  - the order of the clues;
  - how the illustration helped the reader.

> 66 The children read and reread the book, and did not tire of the same clues. They played the game over and over.
> —*Grade 3 teacher* 99

- Encourage the children to take a copy of the small book home to share with members of the family.

Investigating habitats

Listing habitats

- List the places where the creatures might be found and match the animals from the book, for example:

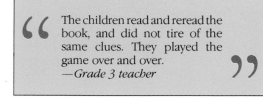

beach:	crab	**flower:**	butterfly
leaf:	spider	**grass:**	praying mantis

- Discuss the habitats of the creatures, for example:
  - The butterfly and the praying mantis would both be found in a garden, but on different plants.

Near a stream

I used to swim but now I can fly. I'm one of the fastest insects alive. What am I?

Answer: Dragonfly

Find me on page 15

10

Children can innovate on the question and answer structure of *Mystery Monsters* (**left**) to make their own lift-the-flap book (**below**). Each child chooses an animal to research and contributes one page to the class book.

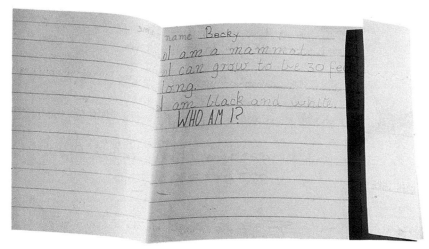

name Becky
I am a mammal.
I can grow to be 30 feet long.
I am black and white.
WHO AM I?

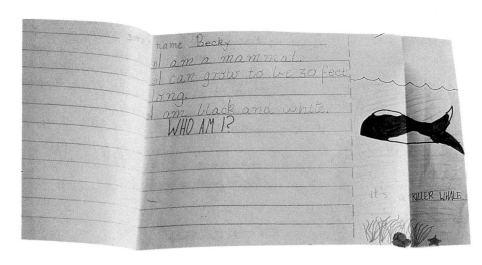

name Becky
I am a mammal.
I can grow to be 30 feet long.
I am black and white.
WHO AM I?

it's a KILLER WHALE

Animal puzzles   35

- A moth does not really live on a window but is attracted there by the light. What is its normal habitat?
- The above list could be rearranged to show all the garden animals, all the sea creatures, and so on, for example:

Beach	Garden	Desert	Sea
crab	spider	snake	fish

Making picture maps

- In pairs or individually, children can draw a picture map to show where some of the creatures in the book might be found.
- The children can report on their picture maps, explaining to each other how they constructed them.

Investigating camouflage

- Revisit the book, and look at the pictures on pages 14–16.

> **Teaching hint:** In rereading the book, let the children find the pages mentioned in the boxes at the bottom of each page, for example "Find me on page 14." Moving between pages is an important skill in reading reference books. Invite individual children to help.

Which animals are difficult to distinguish? Discuss why. Children may like to discuss questions such as the following:

- How do animals disguise themselves?
- Why do animals disguise themselves?
- In what other ways do animals protect themselves from predators?

> **Compare texts:** *Hidden Animals* looks at camouflage in more detail.

Mathematics

- Children estimate the size of the animals. In small groups, children look at the small books together, writing down each animal's name and their estimate of its size. This can be in standard units of measurement (inches, cm), or in more general terms, e.g. "smaller than a snail," "bigger than a flea."
- Children compare the close-up picture of the animal with the whole picture in the answers. They may wish to change their estimates. Ask them to record both their initial and revised estimates before they go to other sources to determine the actual size.

Classification

- Ask the children, working in small groups and using the small books, to list all the creatures and then classify them.
- Compare the children's classifications, and ask them to justify their decisions to the class.
- Ask the children how they could use their classification to help them find out more about the creatures. Discuss which classification systems are more helpful for this.

> **Teaching hint:** Classifying into "animals I like" and "animals I don't like" is not helpful, whereas classifying them as "insects," "spiders," etc., or by habitat is more useful.
>
> Younger children could classify the animals simply on the basis of the number of legs, while older children might be able to use categories such as "invertebrate" or "crustacean."

Research

- The children research either *the creatures in this book* or *other animals*.

The creatures in this book

- Ask the children in small groups to choose one or more of the creatures and write some questions which they would like to answer about the animal.
- The children can use reference books to help them answer their questions. Some of the insects and spiders may be found near the school.
- The children can present their material in a variety of formats, for example:
  - the puzzle format of *Creature Features*;
  - a life cycle diagram as in *Caterpillar Diary* or *Tadpole Diary*;
  - "mystery facts" as in *The Life of the Butterfly*;
  - information statements as in *The Book of Animal Records*.

Other animals

- Using the book *Mystery Monsters* as a model, children can choose another creature and work in pairs to research a mystery monster. They will need to have access to well illustrated books on small animals.
- They can find out three important facts about the animal to use as clues. The structure of "three important facts" gives children the opportunity to focus on the main features of the animal. It helps them to develop the skill of skimming, i.e. it is not always necessary

to read all the information presented.

- The children can draw pictures, or cut up pictures from magazines and pamphlets to illustrate their mystery monsters. If they observe the creature directly, they can use magnifying glasses to help them draw close-up pictures.

- The individual pages produced by each child can be combined to make a class Mystery Monster book, which the children can share with other classes and take home to share with their families.

 The research which went into the class book was extensive. The book the children made does not reveal the process of research, the purpose with which children went about their task, or the decision-making in the final presentation.
—*Grade 3 teacher*

Mixed-up Monsters

Matching the cards (Shuffle and match)

- Write a clue about each animal on a separate index card. Pairs of children shuffle these and match each clue card to an animal. They will need to check their answers with the small books.

Making new cards

- The children can extend this game by making additional cards, based on the creatures in the book or those they have researched for the class book.

Board game (back cover)

- The "Mystery Monster Game" on the back cover of the book is best played on a table or on the floor with four children using the big book. The small books can be used to check the facts.

The children enjoyed playing the game very much and made up their own rules for how to end the game and other rules. For example: 'if you don't get it right the first time, it's the next person's turn.'
—*Grade 3 teacher*

Other mysteries

- Ask the children to bring a variety of plant material: leaves, flowers, fruit, bark, etc.

- Ask the children, in small groups, to examine the items and write down what they see.

- Now ask them to examine the same items through a magnifying glass and make notes about what they see.

- In pairs, children can choose one item and
  - draw the item;
  - draw the item as seen through a magnifying glass;
  - describe any differences between the two views.

The worksheet "Before and After" (page 120 below) will assist the children when recording their information.

- Make a class mural of the children's drawings and writings.

Links with other Informazing books

page 5	spider	*Animal Clues,* pp. 15–16 *Animal Acrobats,* p. 13 *Creature Features,* pp. 3–4
page 6	butterfly	*The Life of the Butterfly Animal Clues,* pp. 13–14
page 9	caterpillar	*The Life of the Butterfly Caterpillar Diary Creature Features,* pp. 11–12 *Hidden Animals,* pp. 8–9
page 13	moth	*Caterpillar Diary Hidden Animals,* pp. 8–9 *Animal, Plant or Mineral?* p. 14
pages 4–13	eyes	Use with *I Spy* for other examples of eyes

Mystery Monsters

Hidden Animals

Animals use camouflage to hide from their enemies, or sometimes from their prey. The reader tries to find them as they hide on bark, in sand, or among seaweed.

Features of the book

Text style	Graphic features
● Problem-solving format	● Back cover flap to hide right-hand pages ● Photographs of animals in natural background ● Photographs of animals separated from background ● Labelled diagrams
Text features ● Predictable pattern ● Question and answer	

You may need

● big book
● small books
● old magazines
● nature pamphlets
● cardboard and paper
● a camera
● scissors
● strong glue

Introducing the book

● Show the children the front cover of the big book, with the title concealed. Discuss what they can see. Does the title help to interpret the cover photograph?

● Read the blurb on the back cover and discuss what the children think the book is about. List the ideas on the board or on paper clipped to an easel next to the book.

Below. Use a piece of cardboard to reveal the clues one at a time, allowing children to refine their predictions as each new clue is added.

Sharing the book: whole class or half class

This book allows the children to draw on their own experiences with small creatures. They need time to discuss these experiences. The children will be able to draw on their knowledge when they write about their own hidden animals.

● Before sharing the book, check that the back cover flap is covering page 3.

● Open the book and compare the picture on page 1 with the cover.

● Refer to the children's predictions about the book. How close were they?

● Turn to page 2 and invite the children to guess what the next animal is. List their suggestions as they are offered. Let the children check and assess each other's suggestions. For example, "It can't be a mouse because mice don't eat leaves."

> " This book gave the children so much to talk about. The children could not find the insect (on pages. 2–3) which provided an excellent introduction to camouflage. The extra information on the diagram was helpful for explaining things further. "
> —*Grade 1 teacher*

● When all the suggestions have been made and commented on, read the answer on page 3. Draw attention to the way the animal is presented:

 ● photograph of the animal in its habitat;
 ● photograph of the animal with the background removed;
 ● labelled diagram.

Use the labelled diagram to explain details in the photograph.

● Invite the children to predict the text on the following page. Use a piece of cardboard to conceal the clues, and reveal them one by one. Give the children the opportunity to offer predictions about both the text and the animal.

Teaching hint: The children's suggestions (which should be written down as the book is read) are an important resource when re-reading the book. Test the suggestions against all the clues, and discuss why some suggestions fit better then others.

Collaborative reading

● If the big book is shared with only *half* the class, let each of those who know the answers have a copy of the small book to read with a friend who did *not* participate in the shared reading. This will give the children additional reading practice with a purpose, and provide positive reinforcement as they demonstrate the book to another child.

● Give the children time to read the small books in pairs or small groups, and to become familiar with the information and the ways in which information is presented.

Library research: camouflage

● Ask the children to find out more about camouflage. Drawing from the information in *Hidden Animals*, ask them to formulate some questions they would like to answer. For example:

● Is it only small animals who need camouflage?
● Why are some animals (such as butterflies, wasps, jewel beetles, parrots) brightly colored and often have no camouflage at all?

● List the information the children have found for later use.

Outdoor investigation

● Search around the school or in the park for small animals which may be difficult to see. Ask the children to list these animals, noting their habitats and sketching the creatures.

● On a field trip to the zoo, the children can observe the camouflage of larger animals. At the beach, they can search for creatures in tide pools and in the sand.

Reporting to the class

● Small groups report their findings (from both the library research and the outdoor investigation) to the class. Make a chart that combines all the new information the children have found.

Hidden Animals

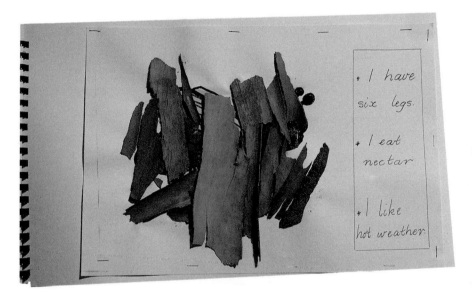

* I have six legs.
* I eat nectar
* I like hot weather.

I am a cicada

Above. Two pages from the children's "Hidden Animals" book show how the original concept has been developed using natural materials.

Animal puzzles   39

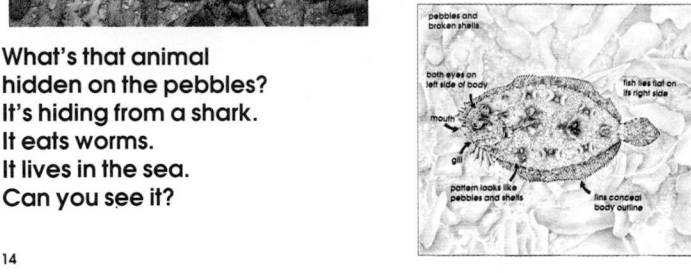

It's a fish.

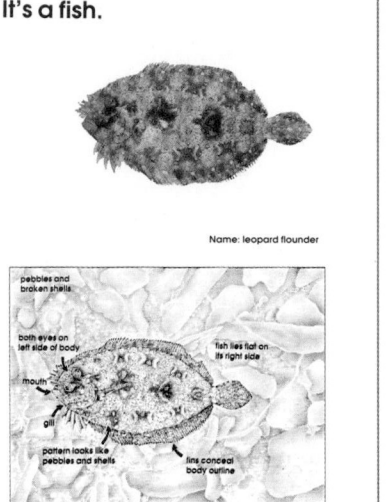

Name: leopard flounder

What's that animal
hidden on the pebbles?
It's hiding from a shark.
It eats worms.
It lives in the sea.
Can you see it?

14

pebbles and
broken shells

both eyes on
left side of body

fish lies flat on
its right side

mouth

gill

pattern looks like
pebbles and shells

fins conceal
body outline

15

Above. Each page of *Hidden Animals* provides information to add to a food web diagram.
Right and below. Working in pairs children build food webs using their own pictures and labels.

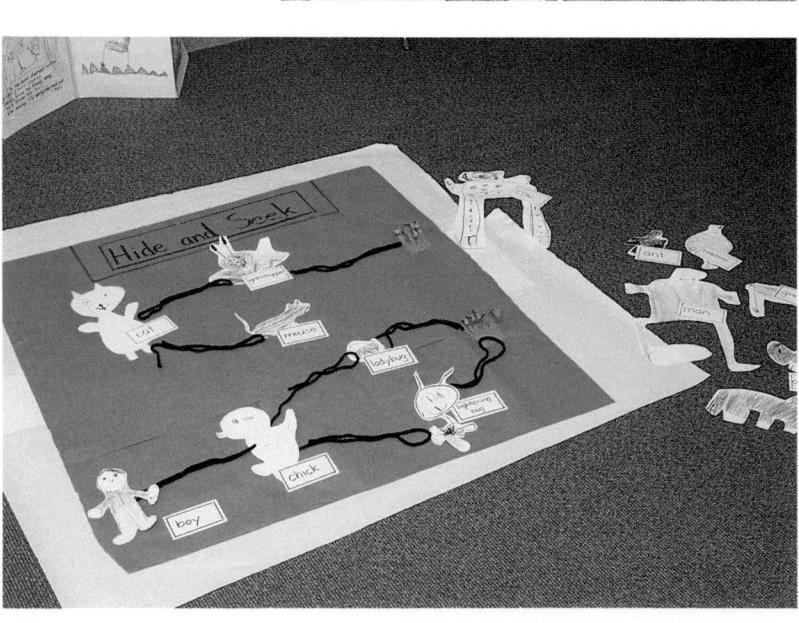

Writing and illustrating

- Using the book as a model, ask the children in small groups to choose an animal and present the information to others.

> **Teaching hint:** The children will need access to other books in order to do this. Even very young children can conduct library research, using pictures rather than text in library books.

- Working in pairs, with the small books and other resources (reference books and the notes they have made from their outdoor investigations), ask the children to choose an animal and to write and draw:
  - the animal camouflaged
  - a labelled diagram of the animal;
  - where the animal lives.

The worksheet "My Hidden Animal" (page 121 below) could be used for this activity.

> **Compare texts:** The children may like to read *I Spy, Animal Clues,* or *Animal Acrobats* for information about other animals. Compare the different ways in which the information is presented.

- Some children may use photographs from nature magazines, tourist brochures, or zoo pamphlets.
- Older children may like to take their own close-up photographs of leaves, bark, sand, grass, etc., and to cut the animal shape out of the background.
- A class book can be made, combining the work of the small groups.

Constructing food chains and food webs

- Each animal in the book is hiding from another animal. Revisit the book, and list the animals and their food, building up a sequence. For example:

"snake *eats* lizard *eats* stick insect *eats* leaves"

These sequences are called food chains.

- Further food chains can be added, derived from the children's knowledge and experience. These can be built up to form more complex patterns called food webs.

Habitats

- List the places where the creatures in the book live. Discuss the link between habitat and camouflage.
- List other habitats and research the cam-

ouflaged animals that live there, drawing on information the children have already gathered through library research and outdoor investigation.

> **Compare texts:** Camouflaged animals can also be found in *Animal Clues, I Spy,* and *Animal Acrobats.*

- The children can draw picture maps of the park, garden, seaside or other area, showing the animals in the book, and other animals that live there, in their habitats.

Classifying animals

- Ask the children to group the animals from the book. When they share their groupings, ask them to justify their decisions. Reference books will be useful.
- The children can add to their groupings the other animals they have observed or read about.
- Discuss the characteristics of groups such as insects, reptiles, birds. For example, an insect has:
  - six legs;
  - three body parts;
  - an external skeleton for protection.

Writing conventions

Making an index

- The children can make an index for *Hidden Animals.* Younger children can focus on just the animals, while older children may include other important vocabulary in the text. Refer to page 33 above (*Millions of Years Ago*) for details on making an index using cards.

> **Compare texts:** *The Book of Animal Records* or *Caterpillar Diary* have suitable models of an index.

Making a glossary

- Discuss the reasons for a glossary, and the style of writing used.

> **Compare texts:** The glossaries in *The Book of Animal Records, Small Worlds,* or *Earth in Danger* will be useful models. Compare the different ways in which glossaries can be presented.

- Make a glossary for *Hidden Animals.* Ask the children (working in a group with the small books) to identify a word which is new to them, and also a word which they think a younger child would not know. Use the information in the book, other reference books, a dictionary, or an encyclopedia to help write definitions or explanations.

> **Teaching hint:** It is useful to read more than one source for definitions when writing a glossary, as dictionaries and encyclopedias give different emphases in their explanations.

- As a class, compare and refine definitions. The final glossary can be pasted inside the back cover flap of the big book.

Arts and crafts

- Ask the children to gather bark, grass, twigs, leaves, and other natural material.
- In pairs, the children make a collage depicting a creature camouflaged by the natural material.

Links with other Informazing books

Hidden Animals

pages 4–5	moth	*Caterpillar Diary Animal, Plant or Mineral?* p. 14 *Mystery Monsters,* p. 13
pages 6–7	lizard	*The Book of Animal Records,* p. 12 *Animal Clues,* pp. 3–4 *What Did You Eat Today?* p. 3
pages 8–9	caterpillar	*Caterpillar Diary What Is It?,* p. 9 *Creature Features,* pp. 11–12 *Mystery Monsters,* p. 9
pages 10–11	shellfish	Similar creatures can be found in *Millions of Years Ago,* pp. 6–9
pages 12–13	grass-hopper	*Animal Clues,* pp. 7–8
pages 14–15	fish	*Millions of Years Ago,* pp. 8–11 *The Book of Animal Records,* p. 13
pages 16–17	bird	*The Book of Animal Records,* pp. 6–8 *Animal Acrobats,* pp. 10–12 *I Spy,* pp. 6–9 *Skeletons,* pp. 6–7

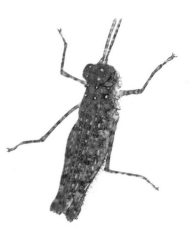

Animal puzzles   41

Skeletons

This book shows a variety of animal skeletons, and gives clues for children to guess "What am I?"

Features of the book

Text style	Graphic features
● Problem-solving format	● Labelled photographs ● Photographs of "answers" ● Fold-out flaps to conceal answers
Text features ● Predictable text ● Text in summary form ● Question and answer	

You may need

- big book
- small books
- a plastic human skeleton
- a variety of animal bones
- *Body Maps* (big book and small books)

Introducing the book

● Show the front cover to the children, which shows a Virginian opossum and its skeleton. Ask the children to compare the two pictures and to "find where the bones would be" in the color picture.

● Turn to page 1 and compare these two pictures of a brushtail possum.

Sharing the book

● Read pages 2–3. Cover the clues, and reveal them one at a time. Allow the children to guess the animal after each clue is revealed. Let the children evaluate each other's guesses in discussion.

● As the clues are revealed, children may be able to eliminate some suggestions or refine others.

> " The children were sure that the baboon skeleton was one of the apes, probably a chimpanzee. When the solution was revealed, the children consulted the dictionary to determine whether a baboon was an ape or a monkey. "
> —*Grade 3 teacher*

● When the answers to both puzzles on pages 2–3 have been read, ask the children to write down something which is the same and something which is different about the two animals. Make a table of these, and keep them for later use when looking at classification. Each page of the book shows a pair of animals that could be compared:

animals	similarities	differences
baboon & monkey		
penguin & duck		
etc.		

● Discuss the special features of each animal (for example, "the eyes and nostrils of the crocodile are on the top of its head") and the purpose of each special feature (for example, "this enables the crocodile to see when its body is under water").

● Share the remainder of the book in the same way.

Collaborative reading

For details of this activity see *Mystery Monsters* (see page 35 above).

Maps

Using the small books and working with a partner, the children can identify the place where each animal in the book is found. Mark these on a world map. The worksheet "World Map" (page 122 below) could be used. The map on pages 14–15 of *The Book of Animal Records* could be used as a model.

Looking at skeletons

Identifying bones

● Compare the skeletons in this book with the drawings on pages 4–9 of *Body Maps*.

● Ask the children, working in small groups using the small books of *Skeletons* and pages 4–5 of *Body Maps*, to choose any page of *Skeletons*. Ask them also to identify features of the leg bones which indicate how the animal moves.

- Compare the teeth and skulls on pages 7–9 of *Body Maps* with those in *Skeletons*. Ask the children to list what they think different animals might eat, and how their teeth will help them to eat that particular food.

Observing

- The children may be able to bring some bones (for example chicken, lamb, or fish bones) to examine at school. They could identify some differences between bird and mammal bones. Why are the bones of birds hollow? (Lighter bones assist flight.)

Classification

Informal classifications

- List the animals in the book, and ask the children, working in pairs or small groups, to classify them.

- Ask the children to share and compare their classifications.

- In doing this activity, and in the earlier discussion of the similarities and differences between the animals on each page of *Skeletons*, it is likely that terms such as

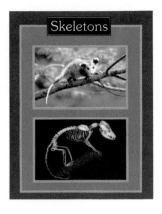
Skeletons

Left. Children reconstruct the skeleton of a cat after studying the photographs in *Skeletons*.

Below left. Allow children to observe, compare impressions, and formulate questions for later research.

Animal puzzles   43

Above. *Small group work.* Two children discuss the skeleton while a third (not in photograph) keeps a list of observations and questions to investigate later.
Right. *Individual work.* Careful investigation raises questions which will form the basis for whole-class discussion.

"reptiles," "mammals," "marsupials," "cat family" and so on will be mentioned. List these terms.

● Other features (such as "furry," "feathers," "live in water," "wild," "domestic," etc.) may form the basis for some children's classifications. List these also.

Animal groups

● Start with the broader groupings:
    ● mammals
    ● reptiles
    ● birds

Ask the children what is special about each group, and how they would decide if an animal fits into the group. Some of the features (such as "furry," "has feathers") will belong in only one of these groups. Others (such as "they fly") will be typical of one group (birds), but also belong to other groups:

    ● bats are mammals;
    ● many insects fly.

There will also be exceptions within a group:

    ● Penguins and ostriches don't fly.

● A Venn diagram can be drawn to show these exceptions, for example:

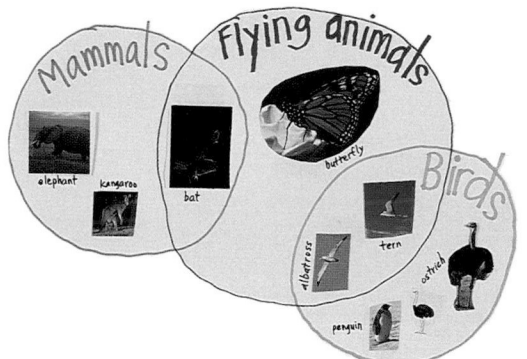

Left. A cardboard skeleton was made by joining the separate parts with split pins. Children can explore how their model skeleton can move. These images were produced by lying the skeleton on a photocopier and changing its position.

Scientific classification

• Older children may be interested in pursuing classification further. Turn to pages 16–17 (the lion and the leopard). Explain how they "fit" into the scientific system of classification. Find their scientific names, *Panthera leo* and *Panthera pardus*:

> • *leo* and *pardus* are their **species** names;
> • they both belong to the **genus** *Panthera*.

Ask the children to suggest other animals which are likely to belong to this genus. They will suggest a number of animals: some will and some won't belong. Not all wild cats belong to the genus *Panthera*.

• Now move to a broader classification, the **family**: the name of the cat family is Felidae. Most of the children's suggestions for the genus *Panthera* will fit into this classification.

• The families themselves belong to an **order**—in this case the meat eaters or Carnivora. And above that comes the **class** "Mammalia" or mammals. Mammals belong to the vertebrates.

Subphylum	Vertebrata (vertebrates)
Class	Mammalia (mammals)
Order	Carnivora (carnivores, or meat-eating mammals)
Family	Felidae (cats)
Genus	*Panthera* (big cats, or panther group)
Species	*Panthera leo* (lion)

The extent of the discussion and of the detail given to the classification will depend on the knowledge and interest of the particular group of children.

Comparing skeletons

• Return to the book *Skeletons* and explain that zoologists use the skeleton of the animal to assist in classification. A zoologist would be able to tell from the skeletons of the lion and the leopard that they are closely related.

• However, the two animals on pages 14–15, the hedgehog and the echidna, although they have features in common such as spines, are far apart on the animal "family tree," and

zoologists can tell this by looking at their skeletons.

• Using the small books and working in small groups, the children list the similarities and differences between the skeletons of the hedgehog and the echidna.

Research

• Revisit the book as a class, or ask the children to read the small books in groups. Ask the children to list questions for each page which they would like to answer.

• Using reference books and the focus questions they have prepared, the children can find out more about particular animals.

The children can present their findings in a variety of ways, for example:

> • as a table, as in *The Life of the Butterfly*;
> • in the puzzle/table format of *Creature Features*;
> • as "mystery facts" as in *The Life of the Butterfly*;
> • as a board game, as in *Mystery Monsters*; or
> • as graphs, as in *What Did You Eat Today?*

Links with other Informazing books

pages 2–3	snake	*What Did You Eat Today?* pp. 8–9 *The Book of Animal Records*, pp. 10–11
pages 2–3	saltwater crocodile	*The Book of Animal Records*, p. 10
pages 4–5	green monkey; baboon	*What Did You Eat Today?* pp. 4–5
pages 6–7	birds	*Animal Acrobats*, pp. 10–12 *The Book of Animal Records*, pp. 6–8 *Hidden Animals*, pp. 16–17 *I Spy*, pp. 6–9
pages 8–9	chameleon (lizard)	*Hidden Animals*, cover, pp. 1, 6, 7 *Animal Acrobats*, pp. 2, 15
pages 8–9	turtle	*The Book of Animal Records*, p. 12

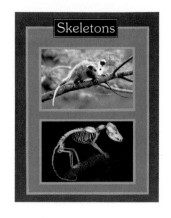

Skeletons

More animal puzzles

The three puzzle books in this section look at details of animals' body parts (*Animal Clues*), the physical features of small creatures (*Creature Features*) and animals' eyesight (*I Spy*).

Opposite page.

Top. The photographs in *Animal Clues* contain more information than the text. Allow children time to interpret the pictures and raise questions about them.
Middle and bottom. Accept all the children's predictions initially, then allow the children to test each suggestion using the pictures, the text and their own knowledge.

Animal Clues

On each page is a puzzle to solve. Look carefully at the pictures and read the clue. Can you guess the animal's name?

Features of the book

Text style • Puzzle format • Predictable text	Graphic features • High-magnification photographs • Microscopic photographs
Text features • Instructions • Question and answer	

You may need

- big book
- small books
- old nature magazines
- zoo pamphlets
- scissors
- paste
- large sheet of cardboard
- colored paper squares
- magnifying glasses
- magnifying containers
- butterfly nets

Introducing the book

Predicting: alternative 1

- Begin with the *back* cover. Before showing it to the children, cover the text with removable adhesive notepaper.
- Discuss the pictures with the children and list their responses for discussion.

> The pictures on the back cover are in black and white because they have been taken by an electron scanning microscope, which does not record color.

- Show the children the text (but not the answers) and ask them if they wish to amend their predictions. Adjust the earlier responses accordingly. Ask the children what they think the book will be about.
- Finally, reveal the answers comparing them with the children's predictions.

Predicting: alternative 2

- Show the children the *front* cover and read the title. Ask the children to suggest what it is they are looking at. What animal might it belong to? List their suggestions.
- Turn to page 1 (the title page). Let the children tell you that the picture shows the answer to the question posed by the cover. Reread the title and discuss the subtitle, "A game for two or more players."

Sharing the book

- Read the "How to play" instructions on page 2.
- Read the book together. Conceal the clues with a piece of cardboard and reveal them one at a time in order to give the children time to discuss the possibilities. Invite the children to join in reading and discussing the text. For example (page 3):

  - "Here is my eye." List on a sheet of paper the suggestions from the children. The children may suggest a lizard, a snake, a crocodile, a rhinoceros, or even a dinosaur.

  - When the second clue is read ("And here are my claws") the children will eliminate the snake and the rhinoceros.

  - The third clue would finally eliminate the crocodile.

> **Teaching hint:** Throughout this process children need to justify their reasons for elimination, for example, "Snakes don't have claws or legs, so that can be crossed off." (Grade 1 child)

- Continue reading the book, giving the children time to discuss each animal, and noting their comments and predictions.

Reading with a partner

- Give the children the small books and allow them time to read the books to each other and to look closely at the photographs.

> This activity gives the children practice in reading and becoming familiar with the structure of the book.

Making an index

- Read the book again, noting each animal's name and page number on a separate card. See the notes on page 33 above (*Millions of Years Ago*) for more details on making an index.

- Ask the children to arrange the cards in alphabetical order. Copy the entries onto page 17 (the inside cover) of the big book of *Animal Clues*.

- Head this page "Index" and ask the children to use it to find some of the animals.

> **Compare texts:** Indexes can be found in *The Life of the Butterfly, Tadpole Diary, Body Facts, Small Worlds* and other Informazing books.

Finding and observing

- Go outside to look for small creatures around the school. Children can make a grass sweep using a butterfly net.

- Examine the creatures with a magnifying glass. Draw them and count and describe their parts (legs, wings, colors, size). The information which the children compile can be used later as a resource for their writing.

- Release the animals where you found them after keeping them for the day.

Writing

Turning graphic information into text

- The text of *Animal Clues* contains only a small amount of information about the animals. The photographs provide much more information. Ask the children, working in pairs or small groups with the small books, to choose one of the animals in the book. If possible, have two different groups working on each animal.

- Using the information provided in the picture alone, the children write as complete a description as they can of the animal. Ask them to use only the photographs initially, excluding other knowledge they have about the animal.

- Ask the children to share their writing. In discussing what they have written, focus on:
  - what in the pictures gave a particular piece of information?
  - vocabulary which helps to describe the features of the animal;
  - different interpretations of the pictures by different groups.

- Now ask each group to add to their description of the animal any other information which they think would be useful or interesting to another person wanting to find out about the animal.

- Using the small books, younger children may do this activity orally in pairs and then present the information to others.

Here is my eye

and here is my foot.

I live in a pond.
I am a ...

11

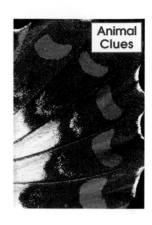

Animal Clues

I am pink.

I have long legs.

I have a beak.

I live in the water I am..

a flamingo.

Above. Eleanor made her own "Animal Clues" book by cutting out pictures from magazines. Two pictures of each animal are needed.
Right. Use a piece of cardboard to reveal the pictures one by one. This focuses children's attention on the detail in each photograph.
Below. Many of the animals in this book show examples of symmetry in nature.

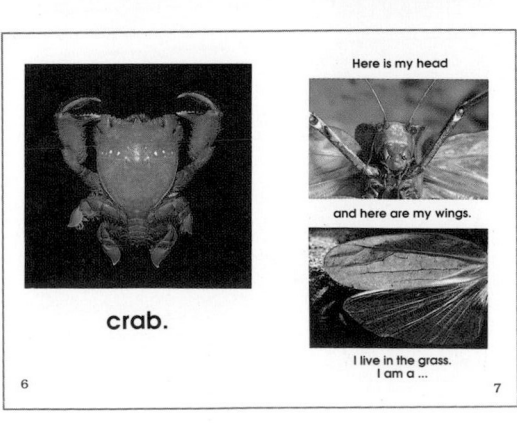

crab.

Here is my head

and here are my wings.

I live in the grass.
I am a ...

6

7

Making a puzzle

● Ask the children to choose another animal, and make up an "animal clues" puzzle about it.

● Before writing and illustrating their own animal clues, the children can present puzzles orally to others. This gives them the opportunity to discuss the clues. For example:

> My nose is long and my feet are big.
> I live in Africa.
> I am an . . .

Discuss:

● Were the clues too easy?
● Were they too difficult?
● Did the clues offer specific information about the animals?

● Search in magazines and pamphlets for pictures of animals. The children need two pictures of the animal, one to cut up and one to reveal the answer. Model this activity using the big book, pointing out how certain features have been highlighted.

● Alternatively, the children can use pictures from reference books to draw the special features and the complete animal.

● Collect the clue sheets and make a class book. This can be taken home for the children to share with their families.

Classification

● Make a set of animal cards (one animal name per card). Each group needs a set. The children could make the cards themselves. This activity provides a purpose for handwriting.

● Ask each small group of children to classify the animals on the cards.

● Have the groups report to the class on the way they have classified the animals. During this time questions can be raised. For example:

● How do the animals eat?
● Which animals are dangerous?
● Where do the animals live?
● What coverings do these animals have?

● The children can make a chart about their particular classifications and illustrate it with photographs, diagrams, or drawings.

48

Exploring symmetry

- To introduce the idea of symmetry, give the children a piece of folded paper and some paints. Have them put blobs of paint on one side of the paper and then ask them to fold it. As they become more skilled they will create symmetrical designs.

- Revisit the book. Ask the children to discuss the symmetry of each animal. Use the worksheet "Animal Symmetry" (on page 123 below) to draw lines of symmetry on each animal. Using the small books as a reference, the children can color the animals accurately to show the symmetrical patterns on their bodies.

> **Teaching hint:** While the other animals in the book have *mirror* symmetry, the sea star (starfish) has *rotational* symmetry. This could be a point for discussion.

- The children can choose other animals and make their own drawings to show their symmetry.

Links with other Informazing books

pages 3–4	lizard	*The Book of Animal Records*, p. 12 *Hidden Animals*, pp. 6–7 *What Did You Eat Today?* p. 3
pages 7–8	grass-hopper	*Hidden Animals*, pp. 12–13
pages 11–12	frog	*I Spy*, pp. 2–5 (toad) *Tadpole Diary Animal Acrobats*, pp. 3, 6
pages 15–16	spider	*Mystery Monsters*, p. 5 *Creature Features*, pp. 3–4 *Animal Acrobats*, p. 13

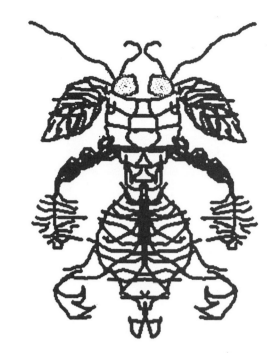

Left. Computer drawing programs allow children to design their own symmetrical animals.

Above and left. Other symmetrical designs can be produced by folding the sheet while the paint is still wet.

More animal puzzles   49

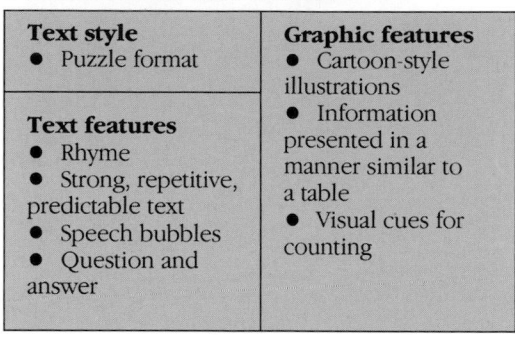

Creature Features

A guessing game which focuses on the features (body parts) of small creatures. You can find these in your garden, at the park, or around the school.

Features of the book

Text style	Graphic features
• Puzzle format	• Cartoon-style illustrations
Text features	• Information presented in a manner similar to a table
• Rhyme	• Visual cues for counting
• Strong, repetitive, predictable text	
• Speech bubbles	
• Question and answer	

You may need

- big book
- small books
- magnifying glasses
- magnifying containers
- containers: cardboard box with holes, or a glass aquarium
- "bug catcher"

Sharing the book

- While reading the book, reveal the clues one at a time. Cover the clues with a piece of cardboard; otherwise the children will read ahead and miss the experience of discussing each clue fully.

- Give the children the opportunity to predict, and to change their predictions if necessary.

- The children may predict bigger animals such as birds and lizards. Ask them to give their reasons. Remind them that the creature has to fit inside the box. Ask them to estimate the size of the box.

Reading with a partner

Using the small books, the children can work in pairs or small groups reading the clues to each other. As well as providing valuable reading practice, the repeated readings familiarize the children with the structure of the text which is useful when they do their own writing.

Keeping animals

- Discuss the catching and keeping of small creatures. Why does the text say "Now that you know, I'm letting it go?" Why does the box have holes in it?

- This could lead to a general discussion on capturing animals and keeping them in captivity. Older children could debate this issue.

Finding and observing

- Go outside to look for small creatures: under stones, among bushes, and on trees. The children can use magnifying glasses and take notes of what they observe. Let the animals go afterwards.

- Some children may bring small animals from home for a day, for instance a pet mouse. The children will need time to share their knowledge and observations of the animals.

- The children can draw and label the animal they have chosen to observe.

Writing "Creature Feature" puzzles

Library research

- Collect as many books on animals as you can, choosing them for the quality of their illustrations. In small groups, the children can list the features of a chosen animal. The focus may be on small animals, or it can be widened to include larger animals.

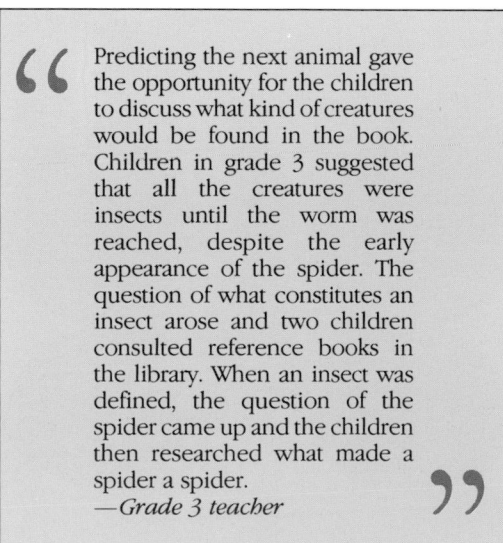

> Predicting the next animal gave the opportunity for the children to discuss what kind of creatures would be found in the book. Children in grade 3 suggested that all the creatures were insects until the worm was reached, despite the early appearance of the spider. The question of what constitutes an insect arose and two children consulted reference books in the library. When an insect was defined, the question of the spider came up and the children then researched what made a spider a spider.
> —*Grade 3 teacher*

Picture research

- The children can count the eyes and legs, note the color and shape and discuss the texture of each animal by researching pictures without being able to "read" the accompanying text. This is a useful way of introducing research skills to five year olds.

Teaching hint: Even very young children who are not confident readers or writers can research all the animal features by studying only the photographs and drawings in an illustrated book. *Mystery Monsters, Animal Clues* and *Hidden Animals* would be useful "picture research" resources for the children.

Focusing on features

- Use the worksheet "Animal Parts" (page 124 below). Cut out the parts and paste them together correctly. Label the parts of the creatures.

Writing the puzzles

- Before writing their puzzles, the children will need time to read the small books to each other and to discuss the pattern of the text.

- Using the book as a model and their own observations and library research, children can work in pairs or small groups to write about their own small creatures, for example:

  - fly
  - mosquito
  - dragonfly
  - grasshopper
  - praying mantis
  - bee

Teaching hint: If the children have already done some work on small creatures, the question and answer structure of this book assists the teacher to find out and assess the discoveries the children have made.

> The activities were used to bring together a unit on small creatures. The oral work and the written activities provided the opportunity to evaluate the learning which had taken place.
> —*Grade 4 teacher*

Zoo visit

- On a visit to the zoo, ask the children to list the features of different animals.

- Afterwards the teacher can collate and staple together all the children's lists to make a book. This book can be shared by the children and also sent home for the children to share with their families.

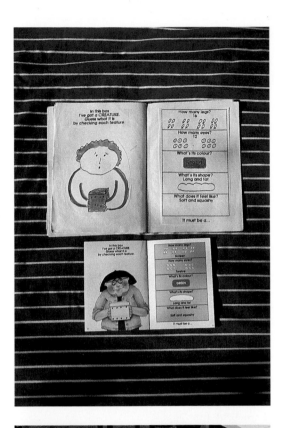

Above left. Let children know that all published books start life as rough drafts similar to their own.
Left. *Creature Features* provides a model for the children's own writing and offers a purpose for research.
Below. Allow children to revisit the book as often as they wish.

More animal puzzles   51

Classifying animals

- Children can devise their own texts using the same structure as *Creature Features*, but focusing on other topics, such as zoo animals, prehistoric animals, plants, etc.

- These activities provide the opportunity for discussion of the classification of animals (or plants). If the class has used animals for creating their texts, they may arrive at groupings such as:

  - amphibians
  - reptiles
  - mammals
  - herbivores
  - carnivores
  - nocturnal animals

- Young children can group animals by one feature, for example number of legs:

0	2	4	6	8
snail worm	bird	lizard	bee	spider

- This would be a good opportunity for introducing correct vocabulary, and clarifying the criteria for such classifications. Some groups are included in other groups, for instance the group *marsupials* fall within the group *mammals*. Other groupings overlap with a number of kinds of animal, for instance "nocturnal animals" include *some* birds, mammals, insects, and spiders. Venn diagrams could be used to show these relationships.

Below. A Venn diagram.

A group of grade 6 children listed insects, and then listed other classes of animals. Finally they listed features, all of which became a resource for their own writing:

Grade 6 Animal List	
Insects	**Animals**
silverfish	mammals
cicada	reptiles
dragonfly	marsupials
butterfly	amphibians
grasshopper	crustaceans
caterpillar	male, female*
wasp	arachnids
moth	human
ant	birds*
ladybird	pachyderm
bee	fish*
dung beetle	rodent
cricket	
mosquito	
flea	
Other Features	**Coverings**
fins	skin hair
sweat glands	scales fur
	feathers

* These items were disputed and discussed: "Did they fit into these lists?"

Links with other Informazing books

pages 3–4	spider	*Mystery Monsters,* p. 5 *Animal Clues,* pp. 15–16 *Animal Acrobats,* p. 13
pages 11–12	caterpillar	*The Life of the Butterfly Caterpillar Diary Mystery Monsters,* p. 9 *Hidden Animals,* pp. 8–9 *Animal, Plant or Mineral?* p. 1

In this box I've got a CREATURE
Guess what it is by checking each
feature.

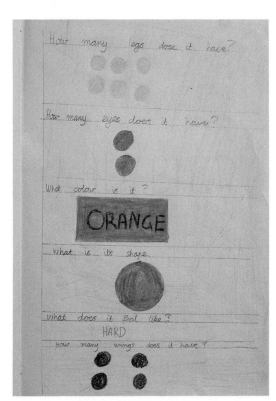

How many legs dose it have?

How many eyes does it have?

What colour is it?

ORANGE

What is its shape.

what does it feal like?

HARD

How many wings does it have?

Creature
Features

Above left. In this innovation on *Creature Features* children have emphasized the mathematics content in their own text about a ladybird.
Below left. In another classroom children have made boxes in which the number of each animal's eyes and legs are represented by blocks.

More animal puzzles 53

I Spy

A book about animal eyesight based on the game "I Spy," which allows children to discover the strange worlds that only animals can see.

Features of the book

Text style	Graphic features
● Predictable text	● Drawings
	● Visual clues to puzzle
Text features	● Peep holes
● Speech bubbles	
● Rhyme	

You may need

- big book
- small books
- large sheets of paper
- model of an eye

Before reading the book

- Play the game "I spy" with the children, either in the classroom or outside.

Teaching hint: Before sharing the big book, read the notes on the inside front cover. These may help answer some of the children's questions when reading the book.

Introducing the book

- Show the children the big book and ask them what they think it will be about. During the reading, list their responses clearly on paper for future reference.
- Read the blurb on the back cover and ask the children if they want to modify their predictions about the book. Ask the children what they already know, for example, "Do cats and dogs see the world the same as we do?" Some children know that their pets have poor color vision.

Collaborative reading

- The book can be initially read with half the class or a smaller group of children. For details about a collaborative reading activity see page 35 above (*Mystery Monsters*).
- The children can then use the small books to introduce the book to other children. This gives the children practice in reading as well as the pleasure of introducing a new book to another child. Children will enjoy taking this book home to share with their families.

Sharing the book

> When using this book with young children for the first time, I focused only on the puzzle and the prediction activity. The children were too excited about the puzzle at first to look at the special features of the animals. But on later readings the children wanted to know more and more about these special animal features.
> —*Kindergarten teacher*

- Read page 2, keeping the clues on page 3 concealed. On page 3, cover the clues with a piece of cardboard and reveal them one by one as you read the page.
- The children can make guesses as each clue is revealed. List these. Encourage the children to assess the suggestions and eliminate some as clues are revealed.

> The children picked up the visual clues, for example for the bird, but didn't get the answer, 'vulture'. They spent lots of time trying to work out what the animal could be before the letter was revealed. The predictable nature of the text offered support to young readers, and the book provided a meaningful context to investigate initial letters.
> —*Kindergarten teacher*

- Read the rest of the book in the same way, allowing the children plenty of time to make predictions and assess the suggestions offered. The children can join in the reading of the predictable text.
- On a second reading, make a table listing the animals in *I Spy* for future reference. Discuss why each animal's eyes have those special features. How is the animal helped by its special kind of eyesight? For example, how does its eyesight help in catching prey, finding its way about, or escaping from enemies?

Sharing the small books

- The children can read the small books in pairs or small groups, and list the information given for each animal for use later.

Below. Ask the children to help you to make an index for *I Spy*. Each word and its page number is written on a separate card. The cards are then arranged by the children in alphabetical order. Copy the text of the index cards on to an extra page of the book.

bee, 17

cat, 13

fish, 21

me, 25

toad, 5

vulture, 9

- The children can read the book to a small group of children, perhaps from a younger class, who do not know the book.

Library research: animals

- In small groups, the children choose an animal from the book, list their own additional knowledge about the animal, and formulate questions about the animal they would like to answer.

- The text of the book will raise questions. For example:

  - How does a toad use its eyes to push food down its throat?
  - What stops the toad from seeing things which are not moving?
  - What is special about a vulture's eyes?
  - What other animals or birds have excellent eyesight?

> **Compare texts:** See *The Book of Animal Records*, page 7, for another bird which can see over long distances.

  - If a cat sees only one or two colors, what are they?
  - What are the patterns that a bee can see in the sky?
  - What are infrared and ultraviolet?
  - Why does the human eye see upside-down?

> **Teaching hint:** Information about these animals can be found inside the front cover of the big book, and some of the children's questions will be answered in these teachers' notes. Others will be found in reference books. The answers to others may not yet exist. This can lead to discussion: our knowledge of the world is never complete.

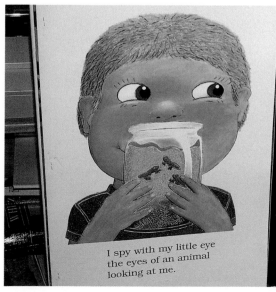

I spy with my little eye the eyes of an animal looking at me.

- It has eyes on the top of its head.
- It can only see things when they move.

tadpole turtle toad

What can it be? It starts with T.

Top. The speech bubbles raise questions that are answered on the inside front cover of the big book.
Above. Allow children to discuss their predictions before revealing the answer.
Left. You can use adhesive note paper to record the children's suggestions. These can be temporarily attached to the page without damaging the book.

More animal puzzles   55

Writing/reporting

- Each group can present the information on their chosen animal, in poster format or some other format. Other Informazing books (such as *Mystery Monsters, The Book of Animal Records* and *Hidden Animals*) will provide models for presenting the children's reports.

Investigating vision

- Children can do simple experiments, for example:

  - **Binocular vision**: hold your finger in front of you and look into the distance; how many fingers do you see?
  - **Peripheral vision**: bring your finger in from the side; when does it appear and disappear again?
  - **Blind spot**: stare at the circle and the cross will disappear.

  O   X

  - **Illusions**: many books of optical illlusions can be found. See also Escher's drawings, and patchwork patterns such as "tumbling blocks."
  - **Pupil power**: stay for a few minutes in a dim room. Look at the pupils of your eyes in a mirror. Now turn on a bright light. Look at your pupils again. They have shrunk. Why?
  - **Make a pinhole camera**: see the notes on the inside front cover of the big book.
  - **Test your eyesight against a vulture's**: see the notes on the inside front cover of the big book.

Making a graph: eye color

- The children can make a graph showing the different eye colors in the class. Young children can count by twos to find the total number of eyes in the class.

Library research: eyes and eyesight

- Investigate the working of the human eye using reference books, and, if available, a model of the eye.

- Investigate further the eyes of other animals in the book, or of other animals the children select. In pairs, the children can make labelled diagrams of the eyes.

- Arrange the diagrams on a large sheet of

Right. After checking his facts in a reference book David wrote his cicada text modelled on the book *I Spy*.
Below. A folded sheet of cardboard with two eye holes was provided for this task.

I Spy

I spy with my little eye the eyes of an insect looking at me.

It has 2 fiery eyes.
It comes out every 17 years.
It lives for one month.

What can it be?
It starts with C.

Right. When sharing the book draw attention to the visual clues on the left hand page (such as the cat collar) as well as the text clues on the right hand page.

I spy with my little eye the eyes of an animal looking at me.

- It can see better than me at night.
- The back of its eye reflects light like a mirror.

What can it be? It starts with C.

paper to make a class display. As a class, discuss the layout and the captions and ask what linking text may be needed.

• Complete the poster by writing the headings, captions, and text and pasting down the diagrams.

Compiling a glossary

• When the children have read the text a number of times, ask them in small groups to identify words they may not be familiar with. Display these where all the children can see them.

• Use a dictionary and look up the words; model this process to the children first. In this way a glossary can be made for the book.

> **Compare texts:** Other Informazing books, such as *The Book of Animal Records* and *Small Worlds*, offer models of glossaries.

Focusing on other body parts

• The children can write their own "I Spy" book, after choosing another feature, for example:

- ears (hearing)
- noses (smell)
- tongues (taste)
- hands and feet
- teeth
- tails

> **Compare texts:** *Body Maps* gives a number of examples of body parts. *The Life of the Butterfly* discusses how butterflies smell, taste, and hear differently from us. Read the "mystery facts" in that book.

• The children can make up clues about different animals, focusing on the chosen body part.

• In *I Spy* the letter names all rhyme with "be." However, the children should not feel restricted to these letters. If they wish to keep the rhyming pattern, they can make up alternatives such as:

I bet you can't guess.
It starts with S.
I'm sure you won't know.
It starts with O.

Writing conventions: speech bubbles

• *I Spy* uses speech bubbles. The children can identify other places (comics, advertising, etc.) where speech bubbles are used. Discuss why they are used here and in other places.

• The children could take another Inform-azing book, for instance *The Book of Animal Records, Hidden Animals,* or *Caterpillar Diary,* and write speech bubbles for some of the animals in those books.

> **Compare texts:** Speech bubbles are also used in *What Did You Eat Today?* and *Creature Features.*

Links with other Informazing books

What Is It?	eye of a fly, p. 5
Animal, Plant or Mineral?	eye of a moth, p. 14
Animal Clues	lizard, pp. 3–4 frog, pp. 11–12 spider, pp. 15–16 ant, beetle, mosquito, wasp: on back cover
Body Facts	lens of eye, p. 10
Creature Features	number of eyes of small creatures
Mystery Monsters	eyes of small creatures

Below. First and second drafts of the book *I Spy* suggest other ways in which the book could have been developed. When children innovate on *Informazing* texts they too should feel free to modify the text structure, rather than copy the book too closely.

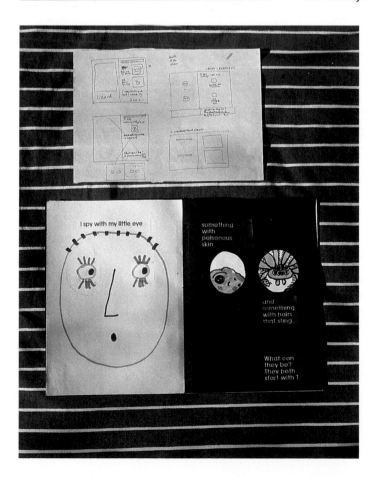

Animal facts

The three books in this section provide intriguing information about animals. *The Book of Animal Records* focuses on records, *What Did You Eat Today?* on diet and *Animal Acrobats* on movement. They provide a range of models for presenting information, and many illustration techniques.

Glossary

Marsupial
An animal which gives milk to its young and which has a pouch to carry its babies.

Migrate
To travel to another part of the world.

Reptile
Scaly animals including snakes, lizards and turtles.

The Book of Animal Records

Find out about the bird that flies the longest distance, the most dangerous fish, the largest bird's nest, and lots of other animal records.

Features of the book

Text style	Graphic features
• Reference book	• Color coding for headings
• Expository text	• Maps
	• Illustrated chart
Text features	• Graphs
• Contents page	• Labelled diagrams
• Introduction	• Scale diagrams
• Glossary	
• Abbreviations	
• Index	

You may need

- big book
- small books
- graph paper
- *The Guinness Book of Records*
- tape measures
- large sheets of paper

Before reading the book

Alternative 1

- Ask the children what a record is. List any records from any field (e.g. sport) the children may know about.

- Discuss different aspects of records.
  - Can all records be broken?
  - What records may never change?
  - Could we set up records in our classroom?

Alternative 2

- Provide large sheets of paper, and ask the children to draw their own pets, or a friend's pet, life size.

- Discuss the size of the pets. Which is the biggest, smallest, longest, tallest? The children can place the drawings in order of size. This could be done in several ways, depending on whether height, length, or weight (mass) is used as the criterion.

- Discuss other features of animals. Ask the children to talk about their pets. Which pets are noisy, funny, fast, and so on?

Sharing the big book

Predicting information

- Show the children the front cover of the book and ask them to decide what kind of records they would expect to find in the book. List these for comparison with the text.

> **Teaching hint:** This is a book for repeated short visits, rather than one long, complete reading. Use it as you would any other reference book, that is, to access specific pieces of information.

Using the contents page

- Show the children the cover of the book, followed by the contents page, and ask them if they can match any of their predictions to the contents page.

- Point out the colors in the headings. Ask the children if they can explain why the headings are in different colors.

- Read the contents page with the children and ask them what facts they would like to discover first.

> This approach to a nonfiction book demonstrates to the children that one way to read an information book is to use the contents page in order to find specific information quickly.

- Turn to the page chosen by the children, and read the entry with them. The children will need time to talk about the records and offer their own relevant knowledge and experience.

Reading the small books

- The children can complete the reading of the book in pairs. They will need time to browse and study the photographs and diagrams.

- During this session the children can also identify any words with which they may not be familiar. These can be listed for reporting to the whole class later and can form the basis for extending the glossary.

Using the glossary

- Turn to the glossary at the back of the big book and read the definitions of some of the terms used in the book.

- Display the words the children listed during their reading and discuss them. The children can consult reference books and dictionaries for definitions, and add these definitions to the glossary in the book.

Research

Constructing questions

- The children work in groups with the small books and construct questions that they would like answered. For example:
  - How do scientists know that sooty terns stay in the air for three years?
  - For how long can the cheetah run at its top speed?

Finding and recording answers

- The children choose one or more of the questions they have constructed, and use reference books or other means to find the answers.
- The information discovered about each animal can be written on cards and attached to the appropriate page of the big book with paper clips or removable adhesive tape. This information can be used later to make a class book about animals.

Mathematics

Posing and solving problems

- Revisit the book, focusing on the diagrammatic information on each page.
- Make up problems from these diagrams. The teacher can demonstrate some problems first, and children can then make up problems themselves. For example:
  - What is the mass of the blue whale on page 4?
  - What is the mass of the brachiosaur on page 4?
  - How many humans would be needed to reach the same height as the giraffe on page 5?
  - How many red kangaroos would it take to match the approximate mass of the saltwater crocodile?
- The children work in pairs and choose their own method of recording and any concrete material they need to use to help solve the problems.
- The children report back to the whole class comparing their methods and their answers.

Largest animal — Blue Whale

Largest animal on land — African Elephant

The largest animal of all time is the Blue Whale which is even heavier than the greatest dinosaurs.

The largest land animal alive today is the African Elephant which usually weighs about 6 tonnes.

A Blue Whale weighs the same as 3 Brachiosuars or 30 African Elephants

human
4

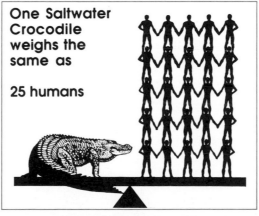

One Saltwater Crocodile weighs the same as 25 humans

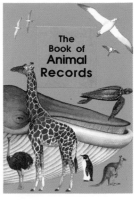

The Book of Animal Records

Above left. Opportunities for mathematics include calculating the mass of the blue whale. **Left.** If a human weighs about 85 kg (200 lb) how much does a saltwater crocodile weigh? **Below.** Children represent the actual length of the python (page 11) using computer paper.

Above. Why not invite a humpback whale to your school?

Comparing size

● The silhouette diagram on the back cover of the book can be used to compare the sizes of the animals and to give the children experience in estimating and measuring.

> **Compare texts:** The silhouettes on the back cover of the book can be used as a model for presenting information from other Informazing books. For example, use silhouettes to show the shapes of different insects, when using *Creature Features* or one of the other books about small creatures.

● After finding the lengths and heights of some of the animals in the book, take the children out to an asphalt or concrete area of the school grounds. Ask them to measure and mark with chalk the length of the blue whale, the height of the giraffe and elephant, and other large animals. If these are all marked from the same baseline, the children will easily be able to visualize and compare the animals' actual sizes.

● The children can compare themselves with the animals by cutting a piece of string the same length as their own height, and seeing how many times the string must be used to equal the height or length of the animal.

● Children can compare their own weight with that of the anaconda, crocodile, African elephant or blue whale. They can calculate how many children it would take to weigh the same as each of these animals.

Graphing

● The children draw graphs to show the heights, weights, or lengths of some of the animals. For height and length, this could be done pictorially.

Writing class books

More animal records

● This book provides the starting point for finding other records in the natural world. *The Guinness Book of Records*, encyclopedias, and other books about animals will be needed.

● The children list records they would like to know about. For example:

  ● What animal lays the biggest egg?
  ● What records do extinct animals hold?
  ● What animal can stand the hottest or coldest conditions?

● Individually children could choose one animal to research further and present their findings in a similar format to that of *The Book of Animal Records*.

● The names of the animals can be written on a world map. The worksheet "World Map" (page 122 below) could be used. Alternatively, the animals' names can be written on small cards or pieces of paper and attached to the map in the big book with removable adhesive tape.

The Book of Tiny Animal Records

● Rewrite the contents page using opposites, for example:

  ● Smallest animal;
  ● Smallest bird.

It will not be possible to find opposites for all the entries. However, the children may think of other entries to include.

● This information can become the basis of a class book, *The Book of Tiny Animal Records*.

> **Compare texts:** For ideas on how to present drawings which show the tiny animals to scale see *Tadpole Diary* and *The Life of the Butterfly*.

A Book of Animal Facts

● The children will have collected a lot of information about animals in their research. Their notes could be written into report form, and made into a class book to accompany the book of records.

Classification

● Ask the children to classify the animals in the book. Compare and discuss their classifications. Discuss what is meant by terms such as "mammal," "reptile," "bird."

> For further information on classification see the lesson plan on *Skeletons*, pages 43–45 above.

Links with other Informazing books

page 4	elephant	*What Did You Eat Today?* p. 2
pages 6–8	birds	*Animal Acrobats*, pp. 10–12 *Body Maps*, pp. 4, 6 *I Spy*, pp. 6–9 *Hidden Animals*, pp. 16–17 *Skeletons*, pp. 6–7
page 9	marsupials	*Skeletons*, pp. 12–13 (koala) *Animal Acrobats*, pp. 8–9
page 10	saltwater crocodile	*Skeletons*, pp. 2–3
pages 10–11	snakes	*Skeletons*, pp. 2–3 *Animal, Plant or Mineral?* p. 4 *What Did You Eat Today?* pp. 8–9
page 12	lizard	*Animal Clues*, pp. 3–4 *Hidden Animals*, cover, pp. 1, 6–7 *What Did You Eat Today?* p. 3
page 12	turtle	*Skeletons*, pp. 8–9 (tortoise)
page 13	shark	*What Did You Eat Today?* p. 6

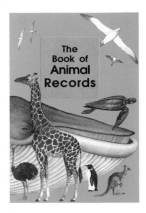

Left and below. After representing the length of a great white shark with the string (**top**) children draw its outline on the school playground, using the string as a scale (**left**). The children also used their armspans as a unit of measurement (**below**).

What Did You Eat Today?

Using a variety of graphic representations this book provides information on the diets of animals in a zoo.

Features of the book

Text styles	Graphic features
● Information written in the first person ● Predictable text ● Puns and other jokes	● Labelled drawings ● Pictograms ● Pictorial tables ● Calendars and clock faces ● Bar graphs ● Column graphs ● Cartoon illustrations
Text features ● Speech bubbles	

You may need

● big book
● small books
● graph paper
● grid paper
● calendars
● clock
● information on nutrition

Introducing the book

● Show the cover and invite predictions of what the book will be about. Discuss the sign in the cover picture: why shouldn't zoo visitors feed the animals?

Sharing the book

The boxed information on the inside front cover explains that this book is based on the normal diet of animals kept in a city zoo.

● Turn to the title page (page 1). Ask whether the children think a tortoise would be given all that food. (Note pages 12–13).

● Read the text at the top of each page, with the children joining in. Allow plenty of time for them to examine and discuss the information and the mode of presentation.

Teaching hint: The reading of this book can take place over a number of sessions.

● The children can count the items in the graphs.

● Give the children opportunities to make comments on the information, such as, "The seal eats four more fish and one more squid in winter than in summer" or "The seal eats twice as much in winter as in summer."

Problem solving using the small books

● The answers to the problems which follow can be found by using the information in the book.

● The problems can be rotated among groups within the classroom. When the children have completed about four of the problems, they can come together and report on their findings. A common problem could be given to all the children so that all can contribute to one particular question.

   ● Which animal in the book eats the most food?

   ● Classify the food eaten by one of the animals (e.g. under headings like "grains," "fruit," "meat," etc). Estimate the weight of food eaten and justify your answer.

   ● Work out a week's feeding schedule for the zookeepers.

   ● Can you estimate how much time any three different animals in the book spend eating?

   ● How many items does one chimpanzee eat in a day, or in a week?

   ● Given the boa constrictor's eating habits, calculate how many rats it would eat in a year.

● The children may also contribute problems for solving.

● The children can work individually or in groups using the small books for reference. Ask them to record their work clearly as they will be sharing it with others.

Rewrite a graph as text

● In pairs and using the small books, the children choose a page, and rewrite the information given in the graph in report form.

Researching another animal

● List the ways in which information is presented in the book (e.g. as bar graphs, calendars, etc.). Discuss this with the children. Is the presentation of the information related to how often the animal eats? For example, look at the bear and the boa constrictor. How useful would it be to present the boa constrictor's eating habits as a bar graph, or the bear's eating habits as a monthly calendar?

Using the frieze: Sequencing and writing a text

• Cut the *Tadpole Diary* frieze (or wallchart) into eight separate pictures. Cut the text off the pictures. The pictures and the text can then be mixed up and used as a sequencing and matching activity.

> **Teaching hint:** Ask the children why they have chosen to put the pictures in a certain order. This activity will give you an insight into what the children already know about tadpoles and frogs.

• In pairs the children choose a picture and write down what is happening in it. Place each piece of text underneath the appropriate pictures.

• The children label as many parts of the frieze as they can.

Sharing the book: Comparing the text with the frieze

• Before reading the book, ensure that the frieze is clearly displayed for reference.

> **Teaching hint:** When pinning the frieze on the wall, make sure the pictures and text are at the children's eye level.

• Share the text *up to page 11* (that is, read only the Diary itself), comparing each page with the text they have written for the frieze. As the two texts are compared, questions may be raised about the differences in the information:

  • Have the children included information that is not in the book?
  • What does the book include that the children have not?
  • Are there any contradictions between the two texts?

• Discuss the differences in the style of language in the two texts. The "Diary" is written in the first person. In what style is the children's text for the frieze written?

Completing the reading of the book

• Discuss how nonfiction books help us to answer our questions about the world. Ask the children if they know of ways in which nonfiction texts help readers to access information. List these for reference during the reading.

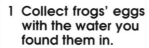

Keeping tadpoles

Why not keep your own tadpoles? Follow these steps.

1 Collect frogs' eggs with the water you found them in.

2 Put them in a fish bowl. Change the water every 2 days.

3 Feed them boiled lettuce each day.

4 Put a stick in the water so the froglets can climb out.

5 Take the young frogs back to the pond. They can't survive at home.

| Week 9 | **Some of our tadpoles have started to grow their back legs. But their bodies seem to have stopped growing. Why is this? We decided to look it up in a tadpole book.** |

Left. Model the use of instructional print by using page 16 of *Tadpole Diary* when you install your tadpoles in the tank.

Above. Children and teacher work together on a text for the frieze which is very different from the diary text in the book (**left**).

Life cycles 79

Tadpole facts

Where can you find tadpoles?

In ponds and pools, wherever there is fresh, still water. Even in puddles beside the road sometimes.

What do tadpoles eat?

Stage	Food
in the egg	egg yolk
just hatched	egg yolk
young tadpole	water weed
older tadpole	water weed, tiny animals in the water, sometimes other tadpoles

12

Tadpole facts

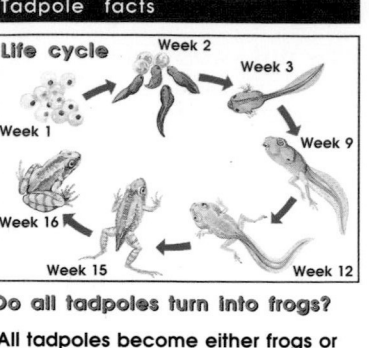

Life cycle
Week 1
Week 2
Week 3
Week 9
Week 16
Week 15
Week 12

Do all tadpoles turn into frogs?

All tadpoles become either frogs or toads, unless they are eaten first. Every tadpole goes through the stages shown in the diagram.

Does the tadpole in this book have a name?

Yes. The tadpole described in this book is called Limnodynastes (say "Lim-no-die-NAS-tees").

13

Frog facts

How many kinds are there?

There are more than 2700 different kinds of frog in the world.

Every year another 100 kinds of frog are discovered.

What do frogs eat?

Live insects, spiders, worms and grubs. Some big frogs eat mice.

Why do frogs have sticky tongues?

Frogs flip out their tongues to catch flying insects. The insects stick to the tongue.

14

Frog facts

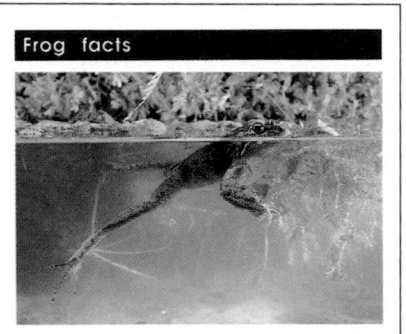

Why do frogs have long legs?

Frogs use their long back legs to jump high in the air, so they can catch flying insects.

How long do frogs live?

Most frogs live for three to five years.

15

Above. The book uses many print conventions such as a table (page 12), a flow chart (page 13), a sequential diagram (page 14), and questions and answers.
Right. In this diagram the pictures are labelled and the labels are defined as in a glossary.

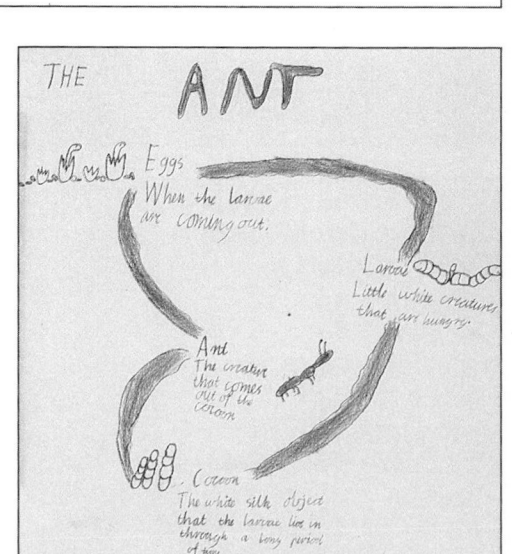

THE ANT

Eggs
When the larvae are coming out.

Larva
Little white creatures that are hungry.

Ant
The creature that comes out of the cocoon.

Cocoon
The white silk object that the larvae live in through a long period of time.

Teaching hint: Before reading pages 12–15, cover the text, leaving only the questions in red visible. This will give the children an opportunity to offer information as they attempt to answer the questions. This information can be drawn from their experience with the frieze, the reading of other books, or their personal experience with tadpoles and frogs.

- Turn to pages 12–13. Ask the children to read the questions, the answers to which should have already been covered. Do the same for pages 14–15.
- Ask the children to choose one question they would like to discuss. In small groups the children gather their information using reference books and report back.
- Finally, reveal the book's answers: read the text of pages 12–15 together, and compare the answers the children discovered with the book's answers.

Revisiting the book

- Read the book again noting conventions such as the scale diagrams, the labelled pictures, the table (page 12), the flow chart (page 13), the photographs, the contents page, and the index.

Comparing illustrations

Diagrams and photographs

- The children compare their drawings and diagrams of the eggs and of the tadpoles at different stages with those in the book. Discuss the differences between the photographs and the drawings.

Flow charts and pie charts

- Show the children the life cycle diagram on page 13 (which is a *flow chart*) and the diagram of the life cycle of the moth on page 16 of *Caterpillar Diary* (which is a *pie chart*). Discuss the two graphic representations and ask the children if they can think of other ways to show a life cycle. The children can redraw the life cycle in *Tadpole Diary* in another way.

Spoken presentations

- Read the text and discuss what Fred sees from his home in the fishbowl (see page 10).
- In groups and using the small books the children can retell a page of *Tadpole Diary* from the point of view of Fred.
- Tape-record the children's oral presentations and discuss the different approaches and the differences in the language the children have used.

By re-presenting the facts in a different style, the children need to find the significant facts which relate to Fred in the original text, and find other ways to express them. To do this the children have to be be involved in reading and rereading the text and understanding it.

Writing

● Some children may like to write and illustrate their presentations. Before they start their illustrations, discuss some ways of presenting these. Will the illustrations be pictures of Fred, or pictures of what Fred sees? Look back at *Tadpole Diary* where the illustrations show what the children saw.

Board game

● Show the children the board game on the back cover of the big book. Allow them to play the game, placing the book flat on the floor or table.

Make a glossary

● Use the index page and ask the children to identify words they may not know.

Compare texts: Models of glossaries can be found in *The Book of Animal Records, Earth in Danger, The Gas Giants,* and other Informazing books.

List the words and in front of the children look the words up in a dictionary or reference book, so that the children have the opportunity to see the teacher model this process.

● The children write a glossary for *Tadpole Diary*.

Making a measurement table

● Using the big book, read the table on page 12 which describes the tadpole's eating habits. Discuss how the information is presented with a minimum of text.

● Look at the life-size drawings of the tadpoles on pages 4–11. Demonstrate, using a ruler, how to measure the length of the tadpole from one of the drawings.

● The children work in pairs, using the small books which also have the life-size drawings. Ask the children to estimate and measure the size of the tadpoles. Ask them to record the measurements and make a table which lists the weeks clearly with the length of the tadpole at each stage. The children will need to do careful measuring.

Teaching hint: Allow the children to design the table using page 12 of *Tadpole Diary* and the back cover of *Caterpillar Diary* as models if they wish. Designing the table itself (rather than just filling in boxes in a table designed by you) helps children to understand more fully the concept of a table.

Observing

● One of the children or your colleagues may be able to bring some goldfish from home. Place them in a separate container next to the tadpoles. Let the children observe and report similarities and differences over a period of time.

When the tadpoles have changed into frogs they should be returned to their natural home.

Links with other Informazing books

Information about frogs	Information about other amphibians
Animal Clues, pp. 11, 12. *Animal Acrobats,* pp. 3, 6	*I Spy,* pp. 2–5 *Millions of Years Ago,* pp. 10–11, 13, 17

Left. Separate the labels and pictures on the frieze and mix them up. Children use the small books to rearrange the elements into a new sequence that makes sense. Alternatively set aside the printed labels and produce a completely new text to go with the pictures.

Life cycles   81

The body

Children are fascinated by the information in these two books, *Body Maps* and *Body Facts*. Because the two presentations are so different, these books complement each other and can be used to compare text styles and print features.

Body Maps

Discover how bodies work by exploring these maps of skeletons, teeth, ears, tongue . . . and brain.

Features of the book

Text style	Graphic features
● Reference book	● Labelled diagrams
	● Exploded diagram (pp. 2–3)
Text features	● Color coding and keys
● Contents page	● Cross sections
● Index	● Enlargement diagrams (p. 12)
● Instructions (p. 2)	
● Captions	● Meaningful distortion (p. 16)
● Boxed text	

Teacher information

● This is a reference book and is not designed to be read at one sitting. Instead, each section can be the focus for a class lesson, in which both the content and the presentation can be examined. When using this book the children should be given the opportunity to discuss the topics and to contribute their own knowledge and experience.

You may need

● big book
● small books
● a plastic skeleton
● a collection of bones (such as fish or chicken bones)
● models of body parts (both animal and human), such as head, heart, eye
● magnifying glasses
● a microscope
● a collection of items to taste
● eyedroppers
● a collection of items to feel

Introducing the book

Predicting

● Cover the title, and ask children what is on the front cover. List their responses.

● Turn to the back cover, and read the blurb. Ask if the children would like to change their suggestions.

● Turn to pages 10–11, which explain the diagram on the cover, and read the text with the children, giving them time to examine the diagram and discuss the statements.

● Ask the children, in pairs, to list what they would like to find out from this book.

● Display and compare the children's lists. Keep the lists for later use.

Body facts

● Prepare a list of questions which can be used to give children an idea of the scope of the book, and to encourage them to look carefully at the diagrams in the book. Questions could include:

● "Do birds have fingers?"
● "What's under my skin?" etc.

Writing

● The following strategies can be used throughout the book and are an excellent way to encourage the children to write.

● How much information can the children write down *using only the diagrams as their source of information?* Any page of this book can yield many lines of text.

● Pairs of children can choose the same page: each child then compares what the other child has written. The information can be collated to accompany the page in the book.

● The children choose different pages and write down all the information in the diagrams. The children can then exchange their writing and extend the information. This can be done until all the children have shared each other's writing.

Investigating bones (pages 2 and 3)

Looking at skeletons

● Show the title page (page 1) of the big book, and ask the children to identify the animal that has this skeleton. Ask the children to justify their guesses.

● Read the note on the inside front cover (under the heading *Page 1 picture*) which identifies the picture as the skeleton of a bat. Allow the children time to comment on the similarities and differences between a human skeleton and the bat's skeleton. Turn to page 4 and show the children the detail featuring the skeleton of the bat's wing before turning to page 2.

- Ask the children to work with a partner to match the bones in the left hand diagram to the skeleton on the right.
- Ask the children to feel the bones in their own bodies and to name the bones they can feel. Amazingly we can feel almost all of the bones in the diagram under our skin.

Word research

> **Teaching hint:** The activity described here can be done as a whole class activity focusing on pages 2–3 of the book. Children can then work independently of the teacher, using the small books, to find out about the words on later pages.

- Many medical and scientific words are of Latin or Greek origin. List these words from pages 2–3, for example:
  - metacarpals
  - femur
  - radius
- Use dictionaries and an encyclopedia to research the origins of the words.
- Match the medical names of the bones to the vernacular (common) names, for example:
  - collarbone = clavicle
  - breastbone = sternum
  - shoulder blade = scapula

Investigating arms and legs (pages 4 and 5)

Using color coding

- Show the children the section on arms and legs on pages 4–5. Ask them if they can explain why the bones in these diagrams are colored differently. If necessary, draw attention to the key in the bottom left hand corner.

Research investigation

- Children may like to investigate the arms and legs of other animals. Or they could formulate general questions based on the information presented in *Body Maps*:
  - What are the differences and similarities between a bat's wing and a bird's wing?
  - Do other animals besides humans have thumbs?
- Compare the different shapes of the legs and their bones. Discuss their function, for example:
  - *bat:* long fingers to hold wing, useless for walking;
  - *rhinoceros:* massive bones, stands on its knuckles to support its weight;
  - *whale:* broad, flat, paddle-shaped; to push through water.

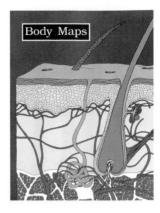

Left and below. Children can compare the bones of an animal's skeleton with their own skeletons using *Body Maps*.

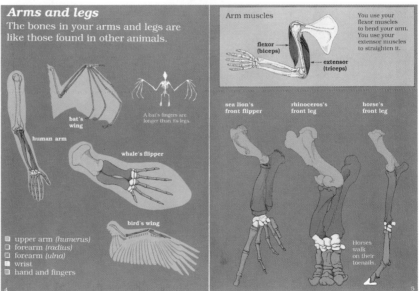

Left. Ask the children to make generalizations from the information they have collected.

Above. Simple charts of information can be produced that combine picture and text.
Right. Children can develop longer texts using the information in the diagrams of *Body Maps*.

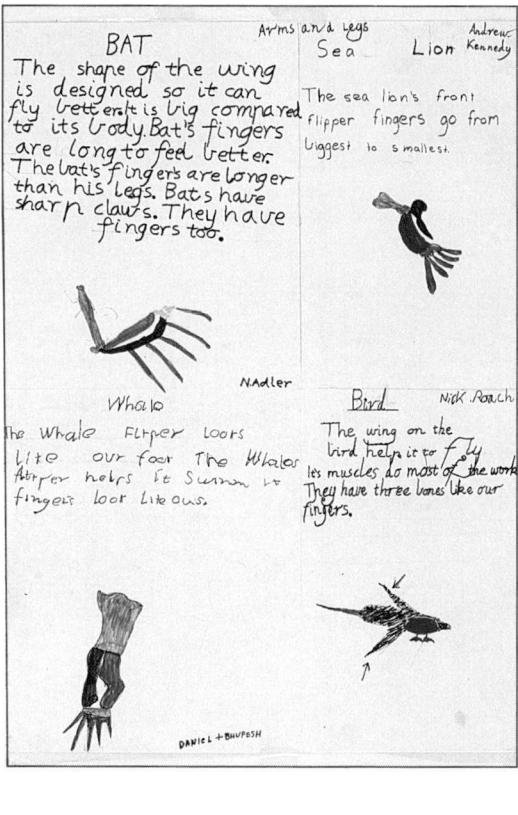

How do arms and legs move?

- Ask the children to move their fingers and thumbs. In which directions can they move? In which directions are they unable to move? Ask the children to describe the movement to a partner.

- Ask the children to move, one at a time, their wrists, forearms, shoulders, then toes, ankles, knees and hips, and, as before, describe the movement to a partner.

- Use a toy construction set to make models of the joints of the arm or leg.

> **Compare texts:** *Animal Acrobats* shows the movement of some animals, and the lesson plan on pages 67-68 above gives ideas for other movement activities.

Hands and feet (page 6)

- The color coding on page 6 is used for a different purpose from that on pages 4-5: on page 6 it is used to highlight a special feature for each hand or foot.

- Discuss the different purposes for each differently shaped hand or foot.

Skulls and teeth (pages 7-9)

- Color coding, cross sections and numbered diagrams are featured.

- Help the children interpret the color coding by asking questions like:
  - Why are the dog's canine teeth different from a human's?
  - Why doesn't a sheep have canine teeth?
- Investigations could be made into:
  - growth of teeth in different animals;
  - teeth and diet;
  - the care of the teeth;
  - what a vet can tell from studying an animal's teeth.

Skin and hair (pages 10-11)

Cross sections and color coding are featured.

- Use a microscope to look at hair, and a magnifying glass to examine the skin surface.

- Estimate and calculate how many times the diagram magnifies your skin: the diagram represents a piece of skin only 2 mm or $1/16$ inch thick.

- Investigate the coverings of other animals:
  - scales
  - fur
  - feathers
  - shell

Tongue (page 12)

Cross sections and color coding are featured.

● Simple experiments on taste could be made. Make sure the tastes cover the range sweet/sour/bitter/salt. Use eyedroppers to place substances on different parts of the tongue. Children decide which column in the table each item belongs in.

sweet	salt	sour	bitter
orange	salty water	lemon	instant coffee
ice cream	soy sauce	vinegar	etc.

Ear (page 13)

Cross sections and color coding are featured.

● Make telephones from cans and string, or place seeds on the surface of a drum, to demonstrate the connection between vibrations and sound.

● Discuss loss of hearing. How do deaf people learn to talk, read, and write? Someone in the school, or a visitor, may be able to demonstrate sign language or lip reading.

Brain (pages 14–15)

The children will need to study the diagrams on the lower part of the page carefully.

● Discuss why some parts of the body send more messages to the brain than others.

> **Compare texts:** See *Body Facts*, page 12, for a picture of brain cells.

Sensitive skin (page 16)

The proportions in this diagram are related to sensitivity, not size. Children will need time and discussion to interpret the picture.

● Compare the picture on page 16 with the brain cross section on pages 14–15. These are two different diagrams that explain the same thing: the more nerve endings you have in one part of your skin, the more nerves you have in your brain coming from that part of your skin.

● Simple experiments on touch can be carried out. Ask the children to bring items to experiment with touch. The children can feel each item and discuss the differences. Describe the items: for example, oily, prickly, sticky, sharp, rough, silky, slimy, etc.

Other body maps

This book gives only a selection of maps of the body. Children can investigate and make body maps of other parts of the human body, or parts of other animals' bodies, using the conventions modelled in this book.

Grade 6 children investigated other body systems, and wrote postcards to tell of their findings:

4 September
Dear Uncle George,
    Having a wonderful time. The people that I'm staying with are really nice. Today we learned about skeletal muscles. They help hold the bones of the skeleton together and they give the body shape. (I bet you didn't know that, Uncle George.)
    Skeletal muscles are mostly found in your arms and legs. Missing you. Say hello to Sarah.
    Love, Jane.
P.S. Hope you are looking after my dog!

Mr Green

11 Grass Street

Greenland 7913

Links with other Informazing books

pages 2–3	bones	*Body Facts*, pp. 1, 3 *Skeletons*
pages 4, 6	bird's wing	*Animal Acrobats*, p. 11 *Skeletons*, pp. 6–7
pages 7–9	skulls and teeth	*Skeletons* *What Did You Eat Today?* (diet and teeth)
pages 10–11	skin and hair	*What Is It?* p. 6 *Body Facts*, p. 11 *Animal, Plant or Mineral?* p. 7

Body Facts

This book answers questions such as "When I cut my hair, why doesn't it hurt?" and shows different parts of the body in color-enhanced microscopic photographs.

Features of the book

Text style	Graphic features
● Reference book	● High-magnification photographs
Text features	● Labelled diagram (p. 17)
● Contents page	● Paintings ("artists' impressions")
● Index	● X-ray photographs
● Questions	● computer generated graphic (page 16: molecule)
● Supporting (boxed) information	
● Captions	

You may need

- big book
- small books
- small books of *Body Maps*
- magnifying glasses

Teaching hint: This book does not have to be read through at one sitting, although children will be reluctant to leave it. It is effective as a reference book or as a springboard for further research.

Sharing the book

Before showing the big book, use a piece of cardboard to cover up the text on page 3, revealing only the heading "What's inside me?"

● Show the front cover of the big book. Tell the children that the picture is a painting, and ask them what they think it shows. List their suggestions.

● Turn to the contents page (page 2). The picture shows blood cells. Compare this with the cover picture. Read the note on the inside front cover (under the heading *Cover picture*), explaining that the painting shows blood cells pouring out of a blood vessel.

● Read the contents page with the children. Allow them time to comment on the questions. The contents page will give the children a way of accessing the information in the book.

● Turn to page 3, where you have concealed the text below the heading "What's inside me?" Tell the children that this page doesn't discuss everything that is inside the human body, but just four important things (such as bones). It also tells how much or how many there are (for example how many bones). Ask each child to write down just four things inside their bodies (and to estimate how many there are of each).

● Ask each child also to write down something they would like to find out about what is inside them.

● The children share what they have written, in small groups of three or four. Each group reports their suggestions to the class, not repeating the items which appear more than once. List these, in two columns:

What's inside me?	
What we know	**What we want to find out**
bones (50?) 2 kidneys blood (about 1 L or 2 pints?) 1 heart	How many hairs on my head? What do germs look like? Why do I blink?

● Uncover the text, and read it. Add the information given in the book to that on the chart. If there are discrepancies (such as the number of bones), note these to be investigated later.

● Ask the children if there are other things they want to find out, now that they have read page 3. Add these to the chart.

Accessing information

● Choose an item the children have contributed to the column "What we want to find out." Ask the children to suggest how we might find out the answer using this book. List the different ways, for example:

- skim through the whole book
- look at the pictures
- use the contents page
- use the index.

● Discuss the different options. Which would be the most efficient for each particular question? When would one of the other options be more efficient?

Using the index

● Demonstrate the use of the index to find information.

Left.

Body Facts uses a question and answer structure to explain some of the concepts that children find most puzzling about their bodies.

Using the boxed information (page 7)

- Cover the information in the box so that only the heading ("How often do I breathe?") can be read. The children predict the information in the box and assess each other's answers. Reveal the information in the box one sentence at a time. (They will want to count their own breaths after reading the first sentence.) Allow the children to revise their predictions as each sentence is revealed.

Body Facts

Contents

What's inside me? • 3
Why do I bleed? • 4
How does the bleeding stop? • 5
Why must I breathe? • 6
What makes me cough? • 8
Why do I blink? • 10
When I cut my hair, why doesn't it hurt? • 11
What's inside my brain? • 12
How big is a cell? • 13
What makes me sick? • 14
How do I get well? • 15
What am I made of? • 16
Index • 17

2

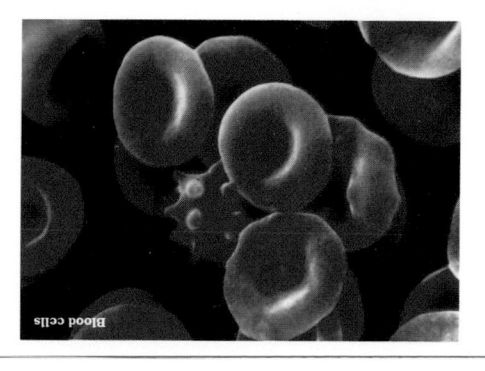

Blood cells

What's inside me?

Inside your body are
- 206 bones,
- more than 600 muscles,
- 96 000 km of blood vessels and
- 50 000 million cells.

☞ You have more cells in your body than there are people on the Earth.
☞ Your blood vessels are long enough to circle the Earth twice.

3

Baby bones
When you were born, you had 100 more bones than you have today. Many of these bones join up as you grow bigger.

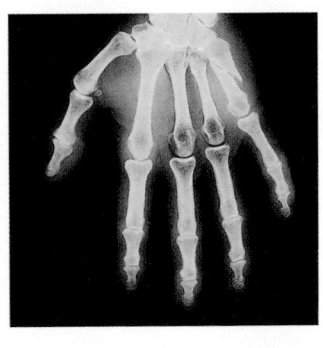

Inside your hand are 27 bones. Each finger has three bones, but your thumb has only two. The other thirteen bones are in your palm.

Research

- Each page in this book offers the opportunity for further research activities.
- In pairs using the small books, children choose one of the questions from the chart they have just made. If *Body Facts* does not answer their question, they will need to consult other reference books. *Body Maps* will also be a useful resource.

Here are some ideas for researching the topics presented in the book.

Compiling a glossary

- In groups or pairs, using the small books, the children can read together and select words to make their own class medical glossary. Words from their own experience could be included in this. The purpose of a glossary and its relation to an index and a contents page should be discussed.

Compare texts: For models of a glossary *The Book of Animal Records, Small Worlds,* or *The Gas Giants* could be used.

Contents (page 2)

- List the questions on the contents page on the board. Ask the children to attempt answers to some of them. Write down the answers in point form under each question. For example:

Why do I blink?	How big is a cell?
• to keep my eyes wet	• less than 1 mm (1/16 inch)
• to clean my eyes	• smaller than you can see
• to keep the dust away	

This activity provides an opportunity to demonstrate note-taking and making summaries.

Using pictures to stimulate discussion (page 3)

- Ask the children whether the x-ray photograph is a right or left hand. How could they decide this?
- Which is the thumb?
- Ask a child to place a hand over the x-ray picture to show the relation between the two. Note the photograph's ghost outline of the hand and the faint shapes of the fingernails.
- Why was the x-ray taken? (One of the bones is broken: which one?)
- Count the bones. Note that some of the "finger" bones are inside the palm.

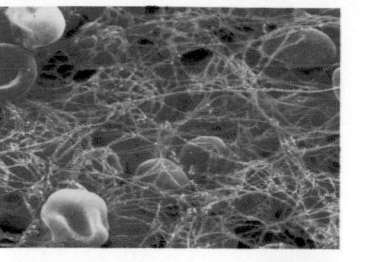

Inside one of your blood vessels can be seen red cells, white cells and platelets. A single drop of blood the size of a pin head contains 5 million red cells, 10 000 white cells and 200 000 platelets.

Why do I bleed?

Your blood is half liquid (called plasma) and half blood cells which carry oxygen to all parts of your body. When you cut yourself the plasma flows out, along with the blood cells. The blood is pushed out by the pumping of your heart.

The heart pump
Your blood is moved around your body by the pumping action of your heart. You can feel this pumping as your heart beating. Your heart pumps 70 000 litres of blood a week. In one day your heart beats 100 000 times.

How does the bleeding stop?

Soon after you start bleeding, some of the platelets in your blood join together. They produce tiny threads at the opening of the cut. These sticky threads form a net that traps the cells so they can't escape.

What keeps my body warm?
Your blood keeps you warm — at about 37°C. Not all animals have the same body temperature. The hottest mammal is the fox (40°C), while birds have a body temperature of 42°.

4

5

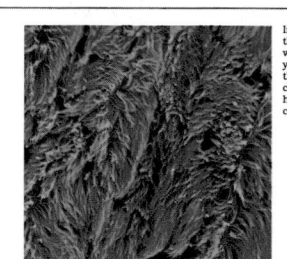

Your lungs have millions of air pockets called alveoli (1). Tiny blood vessels called capillaries form a net around each air pocket. Fresh air is carried to them by small tubes called bronchioles (2).

Why must I breathe?

Every time you breathe in, your lungs fill with air. One-fifth of the air is oxygen. Millions of air pockets in your lungs pass the oxygen into your blood ...

How big are my lungs?
Your lungs hold enough air to fill about eight milk bottles (for five litres). Each lung is folded into a small space inside your chest. But if you spread them out, your lungs would cover a tennis court.

Inside your throat is your windpipe. Inside your windpipe the walls are covered with fine hairs like a carpet.

The blood then carries the oxygen to your muscles, which use up the oxygen when they work for you. Without oxygen your body would stop working.

How often do I breathe?
Count the number of normal breaths you take in one minute. Most people take about 12 breaths in that time. This means you breathe in 17 000 times a day, or more than 6 million times a year.

6

7

Above and right.
Most of the photographs in *Body Facts* are taken with a scanning electron microscope and have been artificially colored to highlight elements in the picture.

In answering children's questions the text uses the impersonal, generalized language of many nonfiction books.

What makes me sick?

The smallest living things are a kind of "germ" that can make you sick. They are the red things attacking one of your cells in the picture. The germ feeds off the cell by breaking it up. When it does this you start feeling sick.

Germs
A germ can be a virus or a bacterium. A **bacterium** is a "visitor" cell that can live alongside the cells that make up your body. A **virus** cannot live by itself. To survive, it has to force its way inside the cells that make up your body.

14

Large numbers (page 4)

● Read the box on page 4 ("The heart pump"). The information about how the heart pumps blood around the body invites the reader to be involved in large numbers. For example, if "your heart beats 100,000 times" in one day, how many times does it beat in one year, or in a lifetime?

● Children will also be challenged by the large numbers involved when discussing red and white blood cells (see the caption at the top of page 4).

Blood (pages 4-5)

● Investigate the body temperatures of animals. Find the animals with the lowest body temperature and the ones with the highest body temperature. Make a chart of the findings.

> **Compare texts:** *Small Worlds* (page 6) provides a model for recording temperatures.

● Questions will arise from this. For example:
 ● How do reptiles keep warm?
 ● Why does a doctor take a blood test?

Breathing (pages 6-7)

● The children record their breath counts before exercise and then after exercise. Why has the breathing rate, pulse rate, and heart rate increased? The children work in small groups and present their reasons diagrammatically. The worksheet "Pulse and Breathing" (page 129 below) gives a format for the children to record their findings.

What makes me sick? (page 14)

● The teacher and the children begin by discussing the issues of hygiene and the place it plays in everyday living. Make a class chart of these hygiene issues.

● The information about bacteria and viruses (pages 14–15) will give the children an opportunity to talk about their knowledge and experience of illness. Such a discussion could lead to children wanting to find out, for example:
 ● What environment is needed to keep healthy?
 ● What environmental conditions existed five hundred years ago?
 ● What environmental conditions exist today in countries in southern Asia, central America, tropical Africa?

● The children's findings could be presented as a letter from a child who lived in the country or during the period studied. Alternatively some children could write the material as a personal journal (modelled on *Caterpillar Diary*).

- The children could consult mortality charts of different countries to pursue this.

> **Teaching hint:** Charts showing mortality rates are readily available from insurance companies.

- Many things which we take for granted are not worldwide:
    - running water
    - sewerage system.

Guessing cards

- The children make guessing cards from paper folded over like a greeting card. A question taken from the contents page or from the boxed information on other pages is written on the front of the card. Inside the card the children write the answer in their own words. The children exchange and collect cards that they can answer.

- The children make new guessing cards based on the research they have been doing. They can exchange and collect cards as before.

Links with other Informazing books

page 1	skeleton	*Body Maps*, pp. 2–6 *Skeletons*
pages 2, 4, 5	blood	*Body Maps*, pp. 10–11
page 3	bones	*Body Maps*, pp. 2–9 *Skeletons*
	muscles	*Body Maps*, pp. 5, 10–11
page 9	pollen	*Animal, Plant or Mineral?* p. 10
page 10	eyes	*I Spy* *Animal, Plant or Mineral?* p. 14 *What Is It?* p. 5
page 11	hair	*Body Maps*, pp. 10–11 *Animal, Plant or Mineral?* p. 7 *What Is It?* p. 6
page 12	brain	*Body Maps*, pp. 14–15
pages 14–15	bacteria, viruses	*What Is It?* p. 16

The lens of your eye is made of millions of flat cells arranged neatly in rows. The ten cells in the picture have been magnified 5000 times.

Why do I blink?
The surface of your eye has a thin layer of skin cells that are very sensitive to dust falling on them. When you blink, your eyelids wash over the surface of the eye with a fluid that clears the dust away.

> **How much time do I spend blinking?**
> A blink lasts less than half a second. But if you add up all the blinking you do in a day, it would equal 30 minutes. So that makes half an hour a day when you can't see anything.

10

Body Facts

Left and below.
Revisit the book to discuss the photographs. Make a chart of additional questions the children would like to research.

These are just a few of the nerve cells that make up the "grey matter" in your brain. These cells receive messages from other parts of your body. They also send out instructions. Your brain exchanges millions of pieces of information every minute.

What's inside my brain?
Your brain is packed with 10 million nerve cells. Each cell has fibres that link it with other nerve cells all over your body. Your brain can think in more ways than the world's largest computer, yet it is 80% water.

> **Two brains in one?**
> Your brain is divided into two halves. You use the left side of your brain when you speak or solve problems in mathematics. You use the right side when you play music, draw a picture or invent things.

12

How many bacteria are at the sharp end of this pin?

How big is a cell?
Your whole body is made of cells. It also contains visiting cells that enter through your nose and mouth. Some of these cells are bacteria — the "germs" that sometimes make you sick. The bacteria cells in the picture are clinging to the sharp end of a pin. A row of at least 50 bacteria cells would be 1 millimetre long.

13

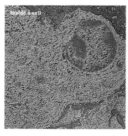

Inside a cell

Inside a molecule

atom →

What am I made of?
Your body is made of cells.
Your cells are made of molecules.
Your molecules are made of atoms.
Your atoms are made of a nucleus and some electrons.
The nucleus is made of protons and neutrons.
And your protons and neutrons are made of quarks ...

16

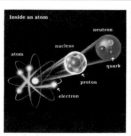

Inside an atom

neutron
nucleus
atom
quark
proton
electron

But suppose that each of your atoms was as big as an Olympic stadium. Then the nucleus inside it would be smaller than a golfball. The electrons would be the size of a few peas. There is nothing else inside your atoms. So your body is more than 99% empty space.

Index

antibiotic, 15
atom, 16, 17
bacteria, 13, 14, 15
blood, 3, 4, 5
bones, 3
brain, 9, 12
breath, 6, 7, 8
bronchiole, 6
capillaries, 4
cell, 2, 3, 4, 5, 10, 11, 13, 14, 16
cough, 8, 9
eye, 10, 11
finger, 3
germs, 13
grey matter, 12
hair, 11
hand, 3
heart, 4
lungs, 6, 7, 9
molecule, 16
muscles, 3, 7
nails, 11
nerves, 9, 11, 12
oxygen, 4, 6, 7
pain, 11, 12
plasma, 4
platelets, 4, 5
pollen, 8, 9
temperature, 5
throat, 7, 8, 9
virus, 14
windpipe, 7, 8
wrist, 3

17

The body   89

Puzzles about the physical world

These two books are concerned with the properties of materials. The puzzle format helps children to develop classification skills while focusing on the solution to the puzzles. Both books provide opportunities for research, and are excellent models for the presentation of the children's findings.

Animal, Plant or Mineral?

This book is based on the game "Animal, plant or mineral" and covers a variety of items from each group. The illustrations are high-magnification photographs.

Features of the book

Text style	Graphic features
● Game format	● High-magnification photographs
● Structured text	● Color-enhanced electron microscope photographs
Text features	● Color-coded text
● Boxed supplementary information	
● Instructions	

You may need

- big book
- small books
- microscopes
- magnifying glasses
- magnifying containers

Before reading the book

● Ask the children if anyone knows the game "Animal, plant or mineral?" or "Twenty questions." Play the game "Animal, plant or mineral?" as an oral activity. Put the rules on a chart.

> **Teaching hint:** Plastic has been invented since this game was first played. As many items in the classroom will be plastic, you may need to add this category. Plastic is an artificial chemical substance made from petroleum and is neither animal, plant, nor mineral. The game then becomes "Animal, plant, mineral or plastic?"

> **Animal, plant, mineral, or plastic?**
> *How to play*
>
> ● One person thinks of an item, and tells whether it is animal, plant, mineral, or plastic.
> ● The others ask questions to determine the object.
> ● The answers to the questions can only be "yes" or "no."
> ● Decide on a limited number of questions, usually twenty, before starting.

● Discuss the style of language which is used when following instructions or rules.

● Record and display the questions asked in the first few games. This will give the children the opportunity to reflect on and evaluate which questions provide the most useful answers.

● After a few games have been played, discuss the value of the information received during the game. Encourage the children to summarize the information before proceeding to the next question. This process makes them focus on the nature of the item, and assists in removing wild guesses.

● The discussion may explore some of the following:
  ● Did the way a question was structured help?
  ● How can we avoid repeating information?
  ● How can we ask "closed" questions—in this case, those with yes/no answers?
  ● What information do we need to know first in order to help us get the answer more quickly?

> **Teaching hint:** Note that very general questions (for example, "natural or artificial?") are more useful at the beginning of the game than very specific questions (such as "does it belong to Emma?").
>
> By analyzing the kinds of questions that are most useful in this game, children discover that the world can be divided into groups within groups. Scientific methods of classification rely on this way of organizing the world. (See also the notes on scientific classification, page 45 above.)

An encyclopedia or dictionary may be needed to decide on some questions raised in this activity. For example, is nylon made from a plant? Is dust animal, plant, or mineral?

> Playing the game before reading the book assists children to think about the information given in each of the clues when they read the book. The discussion during and after the game is extremely valuable. The interaction among the children is as important as that between the teacher and the children.

Sharing the book: reading and talking together

> **Teaching hint:** Conceal all the clues with paper and removable adhesive tape before sharing the book. Otherwise use the piece of cardboard supplied with the big book.

● Show the front cover to the children. Ask the children what they think the picture might

90

be. List their responses on the board or on a large sheet of paper.

● Read the information "A note on the photographs" on the inside front cover. Ask the children if they would like to change their predictions.

Grade 6 children made the following predictions about the picture on the front cover. After reading the "Note" they eliminated some of the answers.

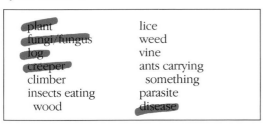

~~plant~~	lice
~~fungi/fungus~~	weed
~~log~~	vine
~~creeper~~	ants carrying
climber	something
insects eating	parasite
wood	~~disease~~

● Turn to page 7. Cover the clues with the piece of cardboard provided, and reveal them one by one.

> **Teaching hint:** Remember to conceal the facing page (page 6) while reading page 7.

● Encourage the children to make guesses as each clue is revealed, and to assess their previous guesses.

● Turn back to the title page (page 1). Ask the children to write down what they believe is shown in the picture on this page. After listening to what the children offer, read the answer on the inside front cover ("Page 1 photo," which explains that this is a caterpillar hatching).

> **Compare texts:** *What Is It?* (page 7) shows a magnified photograph of butterfly eggs, one of which is breaking open.

● Read through the book, following the same procedure as for page 7. Give the children plenty of time to respond to each item.

Classification

● Give the small books to the children and ask them to work in pairs or small groups. Assign each group a category: animal, plant, or mineral. Ask the children to list the appropriate items for their group from the book.

● Ask the children to list any similarities and differences between the items they have found. For example:

> ● *Animal:* all the animal items in the book are parts of living animals.

● Ask the question: "What makes something animal, plant, mineral, or plastic?"

It is part of an animal.
It is getting washed.
There are thousands of them on your head.
The green parts come out of a bottle. It is:

ANSWER: A human hair with shampoo on it.

Enlarged one thousand times, this human hair looks like a tree trunk. There are more than one hundred thousand hairs on your head.

7

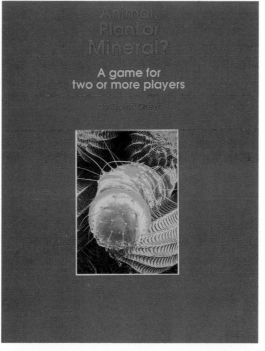

Animal, Plant or Mineral?

A game for two or more players

By David Drew

Everything in this book is either an animal, a plant or a mineral.

You can play a guessing game using this book with one or more friends.

Cover the clues with a piece of cardboard and reveal them one at a time.

Animal, Plant or Mineral?

Above left. Reveal the clues one at a time with a piece of cardboard, allowing the children to offer as many predictions as they wish. As each clue is revealed, ask the children if they wish to change their predictions.
Left and below left. Children benefit from playing the game before reading the book.

Observing items under a microscope

- The children gather some of the items in the book, and others, to examine under the microscope, for example:

  - the petal of a flower
  - a piece of cotton wool
  - a human hair
  - part of a feather
  - tissue paper
  - a thread

> **Teaching hint:** If younger children have difficulty using a microscope, they can use magnifying glasses instead.

After examination, the children draw the items and label their drawings.

> **Compare texts:** *Hidden Animals* offers a model for labelling diagrams.

Writing clues

- The children write clues for the items they have drawn, using the book as a model.

- The children can then find out one additional fact about the item, and use it to complete their puzzle.

- Before writing their final copy, the children should try their puzzle on others, to assess whether their clues are accurate and not too easy or too difficult.

Below. Allow the children time to discuss each clue fully before revealing the next clue. You can record their predictions on a sheet taped to the page. On the first reading you may wish to conceal all the text and to discuss only the pictures.

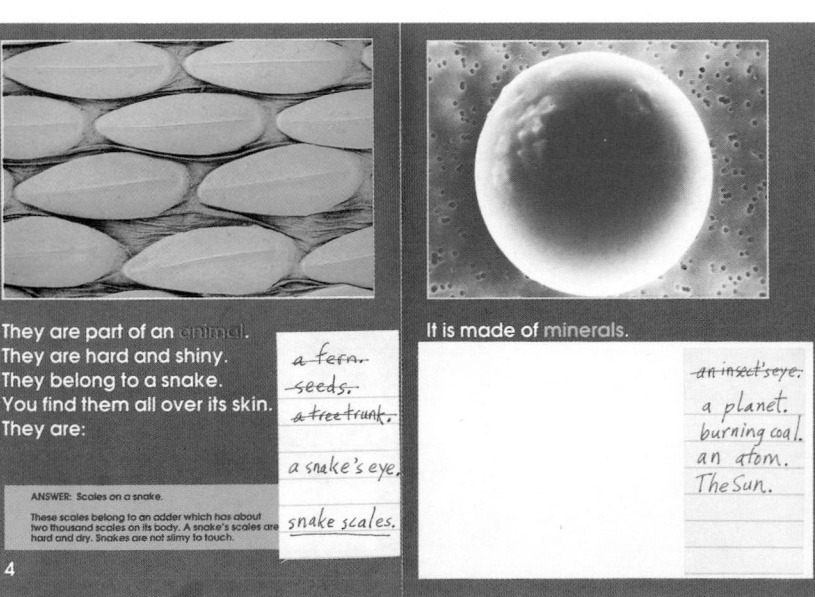

They are part of an animal.
They are hard and shiny.
They belong to a snake.
You find them all over its skin.
They are:

a snake's eye.

ANSWER: Scales on a snake.

These scales belong to an adder which has about two thousand scales on its body. A snake's scales are hard and dry. Snakes are not slimy to touch.

a fern.
seeds.
a tree trunk.

snake scales.

4

It is made of minerals.

an insect's eye.
a planet.
burning coal.
an atom.
The Sun.

Two grade 6 children expressed their clues for the same object in different ways:

It is hard.	I was formed millions of years ago.
It is valuable.	I am made out of carbon.
It is very enduring.	I can glow.
It is made from carbon.	I have eight sides.
It has eight sides.	I come in four different colors.
It was formed millions of years ago.	I am very enduring.
It must be used to cut each other.	I am made deep in the Earth.
It won't dissolve in acid.	I refract light.
It can glow.	
Answer: Diamond	

- A class book can be made of puzzles such as these. The puzzles provide a stimulus for library research and can be used with another class or taken home to share with their families.

- Read the big book *What Is It?* Rewrite the clues using the categories animal, plant, mineral, and plastic.

- Still in their small groups, ask the children to classify items in the classroom as animal, plant, mineral, or plastic.

- The children compare their lists, and discuss any contradictions or differences. Encourage them to justify and talk through their choices before going to the encyclopedia or dictionary to check the items.

Researching information

- The children, in pairs with the small books, reread the clues and the additional information about each item.

Constructing questions

- Each pair of children chooses an item for research, and makes up a question about it which they would like answered. For example:

  - How many scales does a snake have?
  - Why doesn't it hurt when you cut your hair?

- When the children have constructed their questions, they may need to go to other reference books or sources to find the answers.

> See *Body Maps* (page 10) and *Body Facts* (page 11) for more information about hair.

Reporting

- The children report their method of research and their findings orally to the other children.

Modelling note-taking

• As the children present their reports, you can make notes of the main findings on a large sheet of paper for future reference. In this way, the teacher can demonstrate how to select and summarize the main points.

• The children can also take notes and use these in a revised draft of their reports.

Links with other Informazing books

page 1	caterpillar	*Caterpillar Diary Creature Features,* pp. 11–12 *Mystery Monsters,* p. 9 *What Is It?* p. 7
page 4	snake	*Skeletons,* pp. 2–3 *What Did You Eat Today?,* pp. 8–9 *The Book of Animal Records,* pp. 10–11
page 5	comet	*Postcards from the Planets,* pp. 3,22 *Small Worlds,* pp. 15, 17
page 7	human hair	*Body Maps,* pp. 10–11 *Body Facts,* p. 11 *What Is It?* p. 6
page 8	crystals	*What Is It?* pp. 12, 14
page 9	butterfly	*The Life of the Butterfly Animal Clues,* pp. 13–14 *Mystery Monsters,* p. 6
page 10	pollen	*Body Facts,* p. 9
page 11	bird	*The Book of Animal Records,* pp. 6–8 *Animal Acrobats,* pp. 10–12 *I Spy,* pp. 6–9 *Hidden Animals,* pp. 16–17 *Skeletons,* pp. 6–7
page 14	moth	*Caterpillar Diary,* pp. 12–15 *Mystery Monsters,* p. 13

It is part of an animal.
It is the size of a pin head.
It has hundreds of lenses.
The animal is a moth.
It is:

ANSWER: The eye of a moth.

Moths have good eyesight and can see ultraviolet light which we can't see. The whole of a moth's body, except for its eyes, is covered in fur.

14

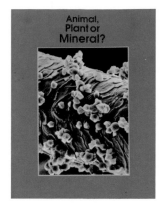

Left. Compare texts in other *Informazing* books. Insect eyes are also discussed in *Caterpillar Diary, Mystery Monsters,* and *What Is It?*

Above. Ask the children to sort and classify familiar objects into categories. This activity introduces children to the uses of a table which arranges information under headings.

What Is It?

A book which invites the children to observe the surprising microscopic appearance of ordinary things. The format is that of a game.

Features of the book

Text style	Graphic features
● Game format ● Structured text	● High-magnification photographs ● Color-enhanced electron microscope photographs
Text features ● Question and answer ● Instructions ● Boxed supplementary information	

You may need

- big book
- small books
- microscope
- magnifying glasses
- magnifying containers

Introducing the book: Front and back cover

● Invite the children to discuss the picture on the cover. What is it? List their replies so everyone can read and assess the suggestions.

● Turn to the back cover. Read the blurb and then ask the children whether they would like to change their predictions. Amend the list and ask the children to explain why they have changed their predictions.

Grade 6 children made the following guesses for the front cover picture. After reading the blurb on the back cover, the children immediately focused on small items. They added additional items, and deleted those items no longer considered possible.

ice	dust	sugar
crystals	soap	boxes
foam	fungus	buildings
salt	carpet hairs	washing machine

Sharing the book: Reading and talking together

Alternative A

● Read the book to the children, concealing the text with the black cardboard provided. Reveal the clues one at a time. Depending on the age of the children involved, one or two children could record the suggestions on the board as each clue is read aloud. The children could then offer answers after seeing each clue.

Alternative B

● The clues on each page are read straight through and the children work in groups or pairs (using the small books) to decide what they think the item might be. The children would need to give reasons for their answers, and these should be related to the information given in the book.

● The class as a whole assesses the alternative "answers" suggested. They will need to use the clues in both the picture and the text to evaluate the suggestions.

Revisiting the book

● Allow individual children to direct a second shared reading. This gives the children confidence as readers and provides valuable reading practice.

● Use the small books for the children to read together in pairs.

> " The children wanted to read and reread these books, enjoying the clues over and over again. This assisted them in their writing. There were opportunities to discuss language which offered specific, new information rather than what was already known or irrelevant. The children also discovered that they needed to do research before moving into writing. "
> —*Grade 6 teacher*

Under a microscope even the most familiar household objects can look strange. But there is a lot to discover when you look at the ordinary world in this extraordinary way...

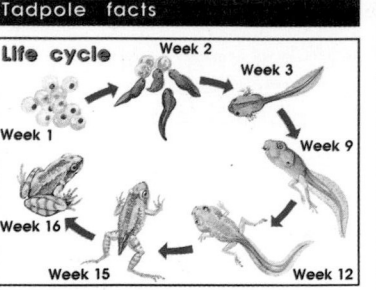

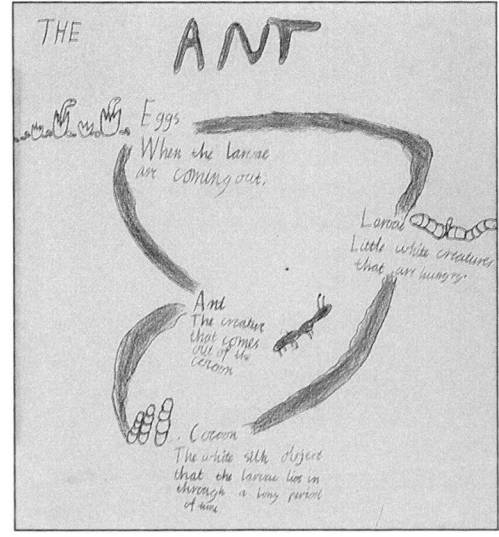

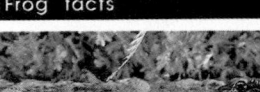

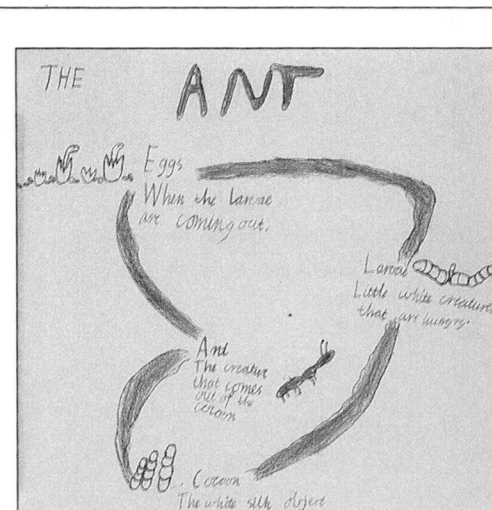

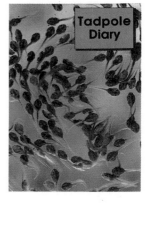

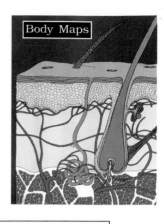

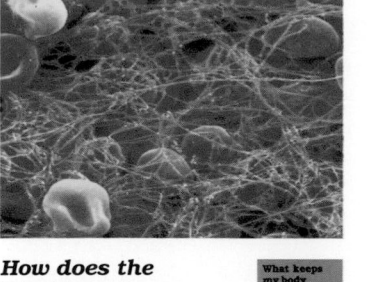

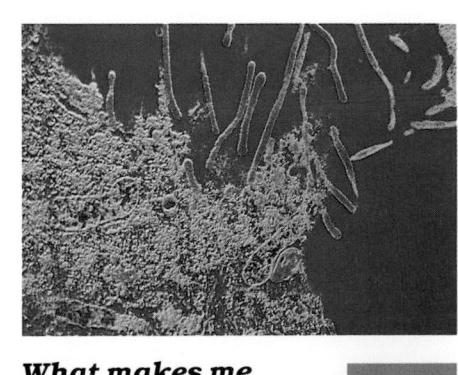

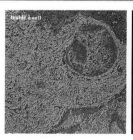

Investigations: magnification

● Set up a microscope in the room. Every few days put something different under the microscope, for example:

- a cat's hair
- a part of a root
- a piece of lettuce
- sugar dissolved in water
- a beetle's wing
- bread crumbs soaked in water
- saliva
- salt

● The children can also experiment with magnifying glasses, or magnifying containers with lids, which are useful for passing objects around the class. Give the children opportunities to talk about what they have seen and to compare their observations.

> **Teaching hint:** *Body Maps* (pages 10–11) includes a cross section diagram of skin and hair which the children may like to read after they have examined their own skin under a magnifying glass.

● The children take turns in bringing an item to examine under the microscope, and having the other children guess what it is.

> ❝ The children enjoyed using the microscope to examine the various items they had chosen. Many of them did their drawings straight from the microscope. The exchange of ideas and information generated a lot of discussion.
> —*Grade 6 teacher* ❞

● Ask the children to compare the appearance of different objects with and then without a lens or microscope. Provide a sheet for the children to record their observations. Divide the sheet in half, marked:

- " ＿＿ looks like this:"
- "Under the lens ＿＿ looks like this:"

After the children have completed their sheets, display their findings and drawings for discussion.

Rewriting information as puzzles

Talking activity

● The children work in pairs to choose an item they have observed under the microscope and researched in library books. They rewrite the information as a "What is it?" puzzle for the rest of the class.

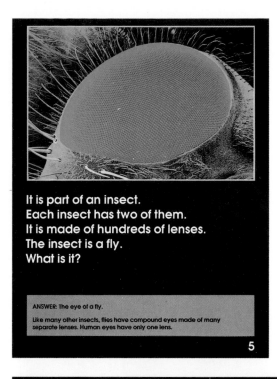

It is part of an insect.
Each insect has two of them.
It is made of hundreds of lenses.
The insect is a fly.
What is it?

ANSWER: The eye of a fly.

Like many other insects, flies have compound eyes made of many separate lenses. Human eyes have only one lens.

5

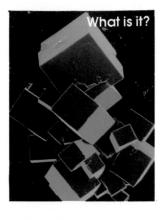

What is it?

Left and below. The children can rewrite the book in another style such as expository text ("A fly has two eyes made of hundreds of lenses ...")

They are always with you.
They can be tiny, or as long as your arm.
There are one hundred thousand of them on your head.
What are they?

ANSWER: Human hairs.

Each hair on your head lasts for about four years. Your eyelashes live for only four months.

6

They are in your garden.
They are as small as pin heads.
You can find them under leaves.
Some of them are starting to hatch.
What are they?

ANSWER: Butterfly eggs.

Every kind of butterfly lays an egg with a different pattern on it. You can see a caterpillar hatching out of one of the eggs.

7

Right. Children should be given the opportunity to write nonfiction in many different styles. Eleanor (grade 1) wrote her own expository text about minerals. Her writing demonstrates an understanding of the generalizations, comparisons, and discriminations found in many nonfiction texts:

Information about rocks

A quartz is just like gold but it's silver. Hematite is black and round. And quartz is shaped like a diamond too. And so is jasper. Jasper is red and blue. Pyrite is small just like other diamonds and shaped like a diamond like every diamond in the world.
Rocks are different sizes and shapes. Some people find triangle rocks.

information about rocks

A Qeozes is gust like Gold But it's selva.
Houmatit is Black and roed.

And Qorsz is sand like a dimoud too. And So is Taspa.

Jaspa is red and Blue.

Pyrit is small gust like ather dimend and sapter like a dimend Like evrer dimend in the wold.

Rocks are defrent Sizs and shaps. Sume peple find triaugl rocks.

- Discuss the results. For example, some clues may have been:
  - too obvious (giving too much information); or
  - too obscure (not giving enough information).

> The skill of playing "What is it?" is to give enough information to create interest and thought, but not so much that it gives the item away at once.

Writing activity

- The children create their own "What is it?" puzzles with pictures from magazines or their own photographs. These can be presented in a variety of ways:
  - *Magazine pictures*: Cut out a small (incomplete) section of the picture and write a clue about it.
  - *Using a camera*: take photographs of objects from unusual angles.

> " On completing the reading of *What Is It?* the children wanted to write and present their own "What is it?" immediately. The children worked in pairs and every child presented clues. Because there had been no research done at this point their responses were in draft form. This activity formed the basis for research.
> —*Grade 6 teacher* "

- The children compile a class book of "What Is It?" from their puzzles. The book can then be presented to another class.

Research

Using instruments

- Telescopes, binoculars, and microscopes have different purposes. List the purposes for which these items are used.
- Working in small groups the children choose an area for investigation, for example:
  - How do binoculars work?
  - Who invented the telescope?
  - Who uses microscopes and for what purposes?

Constructing questions

- The children work in groups using the small books. Ask them to list questions about the pictures in the book that they would like to investigate. These should be questions that are not answered in the book. For example:

- What is a long-playing record made of? What is the difference between a long-playing record and a compact disc?
- Why does rain fall in separate drops?
- Who invented Velcro? Why do they use it on space suits?
- Why do crystals look like blocks?

Modelling research

- Take one picture and ask one question about it. For example:
  - Why do insects have compound eyes made of separate lenses?
- Discuss with the children what headings they will need to look under to find the information in a reference book or a resource such as a museum. For example:
  - begin with *insects*;
  - then look for *eyes* of insects;
  - then look for *lenses* of eyes;
  - scan the text asking "what are they for?"
- Ask the children:
  - What kind of books would have this information?
  - What headings would there be?
  - Which department in the local natural history museum could assist you?
- Invite a librarian to discuss subject headings and the use of a system of classification for libraries.

Answering the questions

- When questions have been decided for investigation the children will need to find the appropriate information.
- From their investigations the children can make a book of "Fantastic Facts" to share.

Growing crystals

- This book shows salt crystals and a vitamin C crystal. It is possible to grow crystals in the classroom, and there are a number of useful resources available to explain the process.
- The children could grow crystals in the classroom and report their observations. *Tadpole Diary* provides a model for a class journal describing such a project.

Links with other Informazing books

page 5	eyes/ eyesight	*I Spy Creature Features*
page 6	hair	*Body Maps,* pp. 10–11 *Body Facts,* p. 11 *Animal, Plant or Mineral?* p. 7
page 7	butterfly	*The Life of the Butterfly Animal Clues,* pp. 13–14
page 9	caterpillar	*The Life of the Butterfly Caterpillar Diary Hidden Animals,* pp. 8–9 *Creature Features,* pp. 11–12
pages 12, 14	crystals	*Animal, Plant or Mineral?* p. 8
page 16	bacteria	*Body Facts,* pp. 13,15

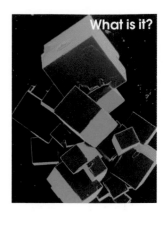

What is it?

Below. *What Is It?* can be a starting point for investigating light, color, technology, health, and the environment, among other topics.

It is a crystal.
It is found in orange juice and in vegetables.
It helps prevent colds.
What is it?

ANSWER: Vitamin C.
Our bodies need vitamins to stay healthy. We get vitamins by eating good food.

14

It lives on a beanstalk.
It sucks sap.
It is as big as a grain of salt.
It is a pest.
What is it?

ANSWER: Thrips.
Thrips are insects that feed in large groups on flowers and the new stems of plants. The long spikes in the picture are hairs growing on the bean leaf and on the beanstalk.

15

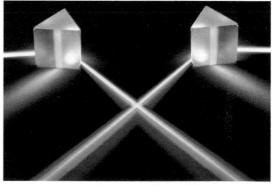

Puzzles about the physical world   97

Space

The four books, *Somewhere in the Universe, Postcards from the Planets, Small Worlds*, and *The Gas Giants*, all deal with space.

Small Worlds and *The Gas Giants* are written as reference books, while *Postcards from the Planets* and *Somewhere in the Universe* provide factual information about the solar system in fictionalized form.

The four books complement each other, and can be used as models for rewriting the information in another form or for presenting additional information.

Below. Begin the reading by sharing the back cover blurb.

Somewhere
in the Universe
is Jason's house ...

Can you find it?

Somewhere in the Universe

Beginning in deep space, this books ends with Jason in his garden, putting the child in the context of the universe.

Features of the book

Text style	Graphic features
● Predictable structure	● Labelled drawings
	● Chart
Text features	● Political map
● Questions to the reader	● Blank map
	● Street map
● Colored text	● Legend/key
● Environmental print (street signs)	● Views from different perspectives

You may need

- big book
- small books
- modelling clay
- telescope
- binoculars
- globe of the world
- atlas
- house plans
- plan of school
- camera and tripod
- local street directory or town plan

Sharing the book

Write in the name of your town or city on the map on pages 10–11 *before* reading the book.

● Show the children the back cover, explaining what a blurb does. Discuss the front cover of the book. Can any of the children name any of the countries, continents, oceans, etc., in the picture?

Picture talk: Jason and the universe

● Read the book to the children. Allow plenty of time for the children to pool all the information they know and all the questions they want to ask about each picture.

● Make a list of the children's comments and questions. These could be presented as a table under the three headings "What we know," "What we are not sure about," and "What we want to know."

● Discuss the pictures *starting from the back* (pages 16–17) and turn the pages until page 2 is reached.

Teaching hint: The "Picture Talk" in the big book is best referred to when information is needed, rather than read out in full. It is intended to assist in answering the children's questions about this complex subject.

● If you were writing to Jason from outer space, what would be his intergalactic address? The children can discover this by working backwards through the book, and can address an envelope to him. (However, Jason's surname is not included in the text.)

Role play: the Solar System

● After reading the book, take the children outside, as plenty of room is needed for this activity. Ask for volunteers or choose children to be the Sun, the Moon, and each of the nine planets.

● Start with the Sun and ask the children to place themselves within the Solar System according to the position of their planet. Give the children labels to wear.

This task creates much discussion. Is the Moon closer to the Earth than to the Sun, or further? Children tend to stand in a line rather than place themselves around the Sun. Other children soon offer advice and information. Page 3 of *Small Worlds* gives an idea of the relative distances of some of the planets from the Sun. Although the differences in the distances are too great for the children to represent accurately, this activity will give them some idea of the relative distances involved.

● When the children are in position, ask them to move around the Sun like a planet. Some children will move around without rotating. Stop and discuss this.

This role-play helps the children understand how the planets move in relation to the Sun and to one another.

The night sky

● Encourage the children and their families to observe the night sky, and identify some of the major constellations. The worksheets "Southern Stars" and "Northern Stars" (pages 130–131 below), will assist in this activity. Provide time at school to discuss what the children have seen.

Research

Investigating space

- The children choose a page from the first half of the book (pages 2–7), and find out additional facts about the topic on that page.
- Ask the children to list two or three important facts using small books of *Postcards from the Planets, The Gas Giants, Small Worlds,* or other references.
- The children report back as a class and put together all their information.

> Asking the children to find out "two or three important facts" gives them a focus for using reference books. It also helps to develop the skills of skimming texts for information, and using the contents page or index as an entry point into the text.

Making a class book

- The information from this research activity can be collated to make a book of information about space.

World map

Identifying countries

- The children find their own country on the world map on pages 8–9. Some children could use a globe of the world. The children label the country on their blank world maps, or on a large outline map. See the worksheet "World Map" (page 122 below).
- Children who were born in another country, or whose parents were, can find and label that country. If they have visited other countries, they can find these also.
- In small groups, the children can continue to fill in the world map worksheet, identifying as many countries as possible.
- When the children report to the whole class, a list can be made of all the named countries. These can be written on cards and used later for a matching game.

Flat maps and globes

- Compare the world map on pages 8–9 with the picture of the Earth on page 8. Compare the map with a globe of the world.
  - What do globes tell you that maps don't? (The distances are more accurate, as are the relative sizes of countries.)
  - What do maps tell you that globes don't? (They often give more detail, and you can see all of the countries at once.)

Somewhere on the grass is Jason.
He's hiding behind the bushes.
Can you find him?

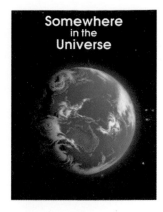

Somewhere in the Universe

Left and below.
This book puts the child in the context of home, city, country, ... and galaxy.

Somewhere in the universe is our galaxy.
It's called the Milky Way.
Can you find it?

The Milky Way

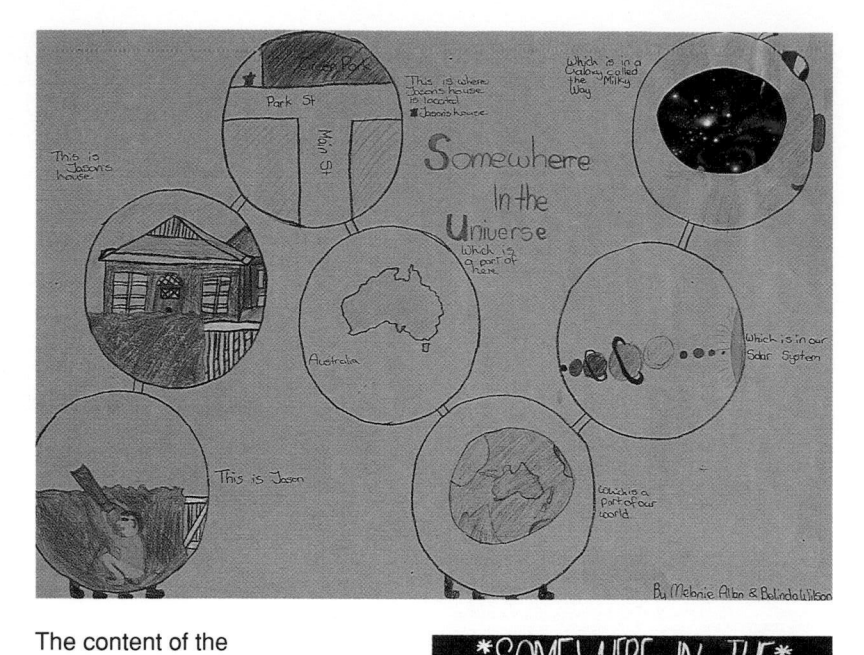

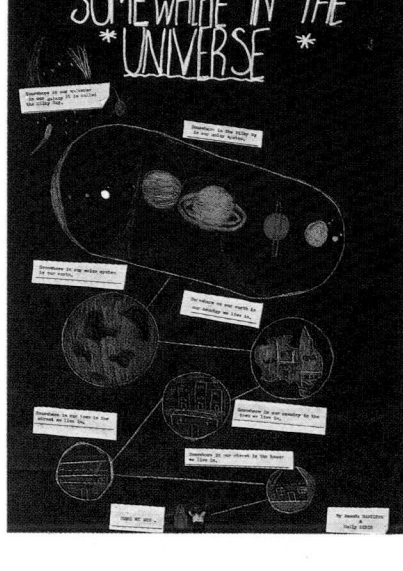

The content of the book can be organized into a sequential diagram. Amanda and Emily transcribed part of the text of the book in their diagram (**right**), whereas Melanie and Belinda devised a new text (**above**).

Below. Hugo drew a map of his daily journey from home to school using conventional symbols (the railroad track) and invented ones (the parks). Children's maps often include details that do not appear in regular street maps.

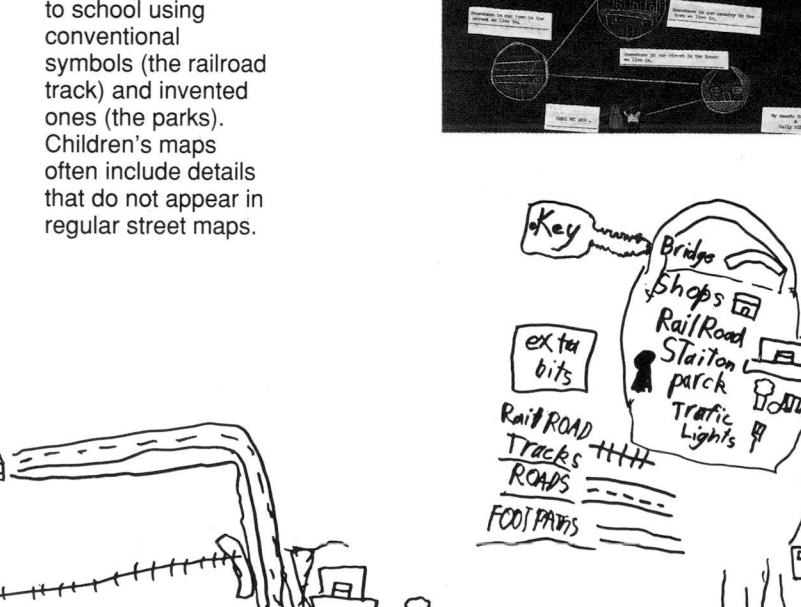

Globes of the Moon and of Mars are available from some shops that specialize in maps. If possible, compare these with a globe of the Earth.

Locations within locations

- As a class, list all the world landmarks children can think of, for example:
  - Great Wall of China
  - Tower of London
  - Sydney Opera House
  - Statue of Liberty
  - Eiffel Tower
  - The Sphinx
- These can be written on the world maps.
- Revisit the book to highlight the way in which each location is included in the previous location. Make a diagram to show this relation for the world landmarks, for example:

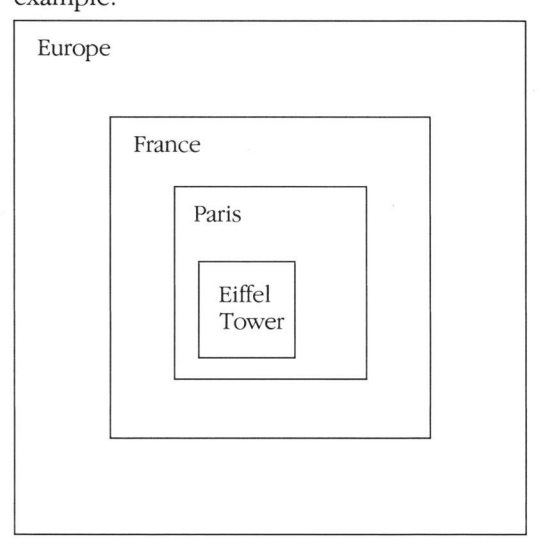

- The children can do the same for other landmarks on the list.
- A book can be developed using the pattern:
  - Somewhere in Europe is France.
  - Somewhere in France is . . . *etc.*

Local mapping

- Working in groups and using the small books ask the children to compare pages 12 and 13 and to make notes of the differences they find.
- As a class, discuss the differences between the bird's eye view (page 12) and the map (page 13) using the children's notes. Why are there no trees, cars, or playground equipment on the map, and why are the map's houses all the same color?
- Examine your local street directory or town map. Discuss the differences between this and

an atlas, for example the different symbols in the legend (or key).

- Ask the children to draw a map of their route from home to school, or from home to a local place of importance to them. Alternatively, go for a walk around the streets near your school, and ask children to draw individual maps of the walk.

- Ask the children to compare their maps with the local street directory. Discuss the differences. What did the children observe and include that was not on the directory map (for instance, trees, playground equipment, shop names)? What did the directory include that the children did not?

Classroom maps

- In pairs, the children can make a plan of their classroom. Some children may like to make a map of the whole school.

- Before the maps are complete, the children can compare their work and discuss the different approaches. They may choose to incorporate some of the other children's ideas in their final map. For instance, some children may include a legend, or a scale, or color coding.

Discussion about maps

- Pose the following questions for class discussion:

  - If a map had *every* detail in it, would it be a good map?

  - If a map were as big as the place it represents, would it be a good map?

  - Can you map things other than places?

Compare texts: See *Body Maps* for a different kind of map. There will probably be disagreement over the question "Can you map things other than places?" It is not necessary to resolve the disagreements, but raising the question focuses on the characteristics and purposes of a map. The difference may be one of terminology: for example, are wiring diagrams maps?

Links with other Informazing books

pages 4–5	Sun	*Postcards from the Planets*, pp. 8–9
pages 6–7	planets	*Postcards from the Planets* *Small Worlds*, pp. 2–3 *The Gas Giants*, pp. 2–3

Somewhere in our town is the street Jason lives in. It's the street beside the park. Can you find it?

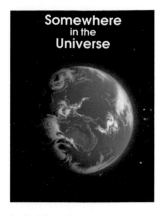

Somewhere in the Universe

Left. How does a bird's eye view differ from a map?
Below. Children can make a map of any place they know well.

Space   101

Postcards from the Planets

Kate and Jessie set off for a one-year trip around the Solar System. The postcards they send home tell relatives about their trip: about both the features of the planets and the personalities of the travellers.

Features of the book

Text style	Graphic features
● Narrative	● Modern illustration techniques:
	● airbrush painting
Text features	● photographic montages
● Postcards	● Postage stamps
● Letter (p. 25)	● Actual photographs
● Addresses	
● Dates	
● Newspaper front page (p. 24)	
● Radio conversation (p. 23)	

You may need

- big book
- small books
- real postcards
- blank postcards
- large sheets of paper
- star maps
- telescope or binoculars
- big books of *Small Worlds* and *The Gas Giants*

Introducing the book

Choose one or more of these activities:

- Send all the children a real postcard.
- Ask the children to bring postcards from home.
- Get the children to write postcards to other members of the class.

Sharing the book

● Start with the back-cover blurb. Then discuss the cover picture and title, and page 1.

● Read the big book to the children, allowing them to enjoy it.

● Revisit the book and focus on text and graphic features. For example:

- On page 2, read the date and address on the postcard first. This helps to establish the postcard's audience. Discuss the stamp and the caption on the postcard.
- On pages 3–22, read each postcard, including the date and caption. Share the address only where a new address appears.
- On page 23, discuss this form of communication: it's not a postcard but a radio message.
- Page 24 is another form of communication: a newspaper report.
- Page 25 is a letter. How does it differ from a postcard?

Further readings of the big book

Fact and fiction

● During a later reading, ask the children how much of the text they think is true. Read the note on the inside front cover:

> **How much of this book is true?**
> Although the story in this book is fiction, the basic information about the planets is true. The book has been carefully researched to describe accurately what it would feel like to visit each of the planets.

Library: cataloguing

● Ask the children whether the book should be put in the nonfiction section of the library or the fiction section. List the reasons, and check with the librarian.

Taking notes: the planets

● As the book is reread, ask the children to list the names of the planets (as well as the Sun and the Moon) as headings on a large sheet of paper:

Moon	Venus	Mercury	Sun	Mars	etc.

● As the book is read, the children add the facts in the text to this table. They may later use other books to find more information on some or all of the planets. This material can be kept as a basis for later research and writing.

Research

Modelling research skills

● Ask the children what they would like to find out about the planets or space travel now that they have read this book. List their questions, and choose one (for example, "Is the Moon a planet?") which is answered in *Small Worlds* or *The Gas Giants*, to demonstrate the use of reference books.

• Show the children the big book of *Small Worlds* or *The Gas Giants*. These provide opportunities to demonstrate the uses of a contents page, an index, pictures with captions, diagrams, tables, headings, labels, etc. With the children, find the answer to their question (see *Small Worlds*, page 2, or *The Gas Giants*, page 10).

• Remind the children that not all questions about the planets can be answered from these books, and ask them to suggest where else they may find relevant information.

Constructing questions

• In pairs or groups, ask the children to read through the small books and list questions which might be answered by reference to other books on planets and space travel. For example:

> • How far away from the Sun are Venus and Mercury?
> • How deep is the Grand Canyon? How high is Mount Everest?
> • What do astronauts eat during space journeys, and how?
> • What is gravity? Why can you jump so high on the Moon?
> • How do we know Saturn would float in water?

• The children can choose one or more of these questions, find out the answers, and present these orally or in poster form to the class.

Writing

A diary

• Using the small books as reference, children rewrite a part of the text in the form of a diary kept by Kate, Jessie, or their father.

> **Compare texts:** You may wish to demonstrate different diary styles before the children begin writing. *Caterpillar Diary* and *Tadpole Diary* offer examples of a personal diary and a group's journal or log. Other examples can be found in fiction.

Addresses

• Examine the addresses in the book. Ask the children to devise some names and addresses for postcards they wish to send. They could choose a friend, a relative, a famous athlete, etc.

The Daily News

31 December 2095

Tourists arrive home by air taxi after their safe return to Earthport yesterday.

SPACE BUS RETURNS SAFELY

Earthport, Monday. — The space ship "Icarus" returned to Earth safely today after twelve months in space. Nicknamed the "space bus", the vehicle travelled to all nine planets in the Solar System.

The 86 crew and 405 passengers are reported in good health on their return.

The captain of the "Icarus", Lieut. Wendy Coolhead, said on arrival that she experienced no in-flight difficulties apart from a girl who was caught raiding the ship's supplies in search of a spaghetti sandwich.

Postcards from the Planets

Print conventions in this book include newspapers (**left**) as well as postcards (**below**).

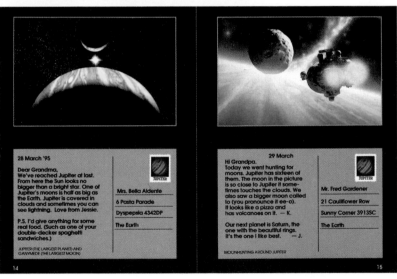

28 March '95

Dear Grandma,
We've reached Jupiter at last. From here the Sun looks no bigger than a bright star. One of Jupiter's moons is half as big as the Earth. Jupiter is covered in clouds and sometimes you can see lightning. Love from Jessie.

P.S. I'd give anything for some real food. (Such as one of your double-decker spaghetti sandwiches.)

JUPITER (THE LARGEST PLANET) AND GANYMEDE (THE LARGEST MOON)

Mrs. Bella Aldente
6 Pasta Parade
Dyspepsia 4342DP
The Earth

14

29 March

Hi Grandpa.
Today we went hunting for moons. Jupiter has sixteen of them. The moon in the picture is so close to Jupiter it sometimes touches the clouds. We also saw a bigger moon called Io (you pronounce it ee-o). It looks like a pizza and has volcanoes on it. — K.

Our next planet is Saturn, the one with the beautiful rings. It's the one I like best. — J.

MOONHUNTING AROUND JUPITER

Mr. Fred Gardener
21 Cauliflower Row
Sunny Corner 3913SC
The Earth

15

4 Easy Street
Hometown 5443HT
1 / 1 / 96

Hi Grandma!
Did you see the photo of us in the paper? It showed us arriving home on New Year's Eve by air taxi. Aunt May was waiting for us. See you on Friday. I'll bring my space rock collection to show you.
Love, Kate.

Dear Grandma,
Everything on Earth is so heavy and I get tired after taking only a few steps. But the air smells nice, and it's warm, and the Earth has got animals and plants — and the best spaghetti sandwiches in the Solar System.
Love from Jessie.

Left. How does the format of a letter differ from a postcard?

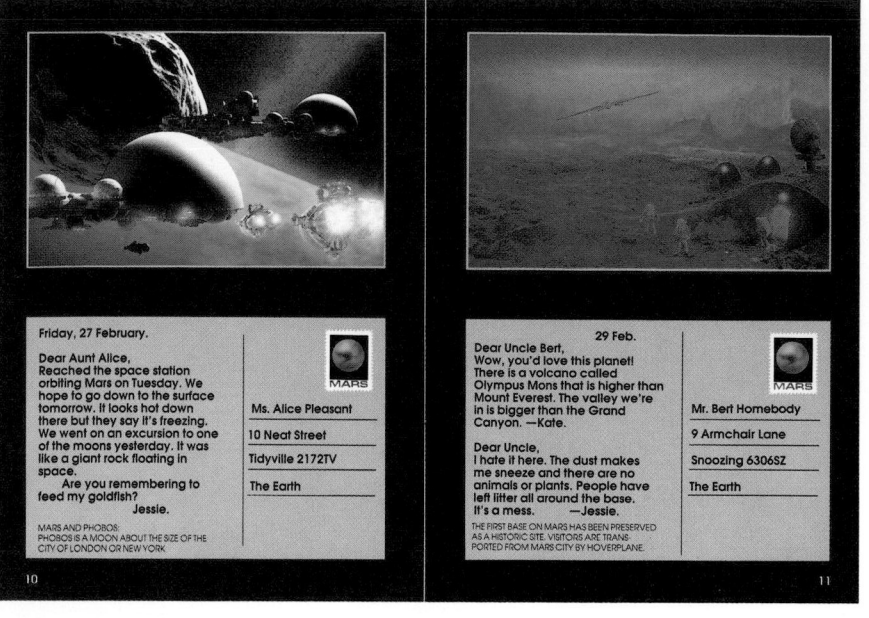

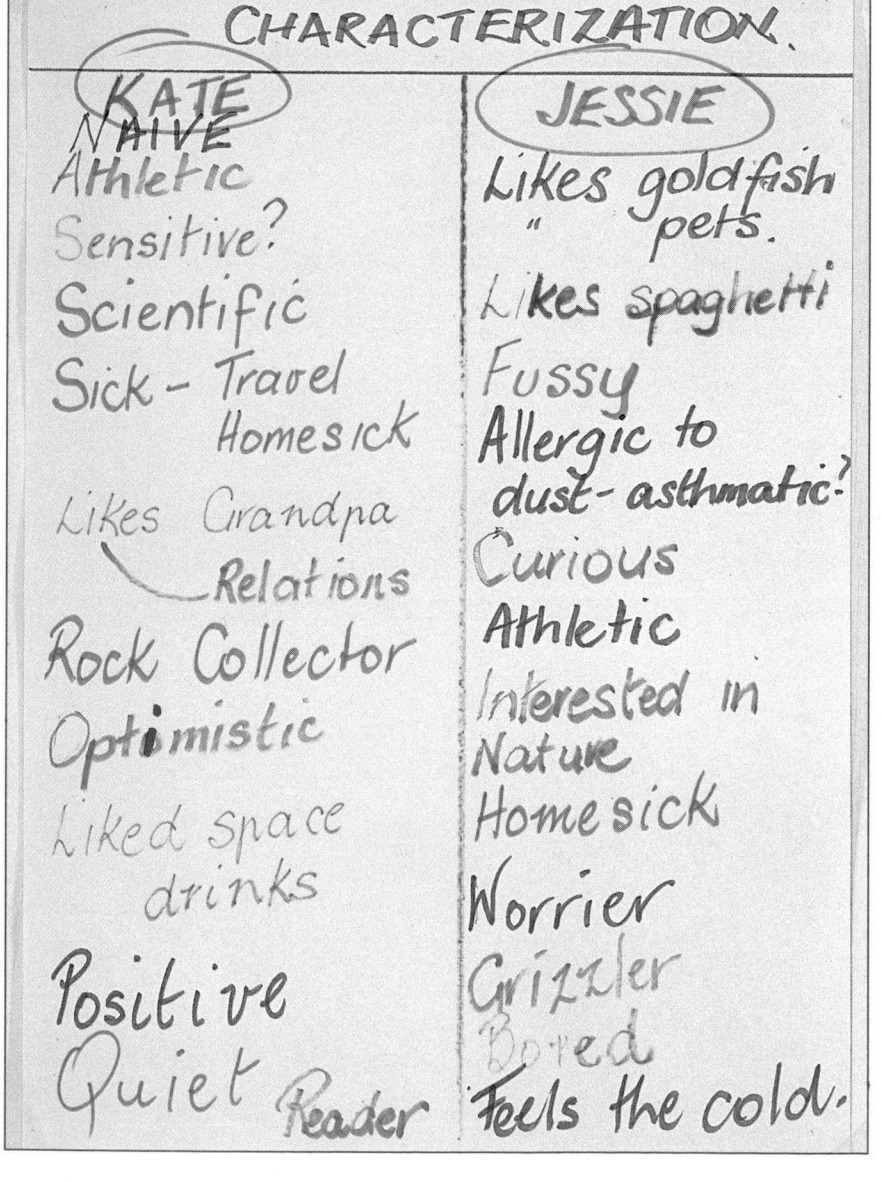

- The names and addresses could be written on blank postcards and the cards could be displayed.

Grade 6 children wrote postcards from different parts of the body after reading Postcards from the Planets *and* Body Maps. *Claire addressed her postcards from the bloodstream to:*

Mrs. Heart 10 Lovelane Road Romanceville 3860	Count Dracula 17 Blood Road Transylvania 361142

Dates

- Draw the children's attention to the different ways of writing the date in *Postcards from the Planets*. Ask them to write today's date in as many different ways as they can. The children should explain each method of writing the date to a partner.

> 66 *Postcards from the Planets* was received with great interest, and provided motivation for research as well as good models for writing. Even children who were usually not willing to write became involved in writing postcards.—*Grade 5 teacher* 99

Characterization

- Divide the class into four groups. Two groups are Kate and the other two groups are Jessie.

- The children in each group work through the small book listing all the clues to the personality of either Jessie or Kate. For example:

Jessie
- thinks the Moon is weird
- worries about her goldfish
- hates litter
- likes spaghetti
- complains a lot

- When the groups report to the class, compare how the two Jessie groups saw Jessie. Were different views expressed? Why? Similarly compare the two Kate groups. Ask the children how they themselves would react to the places and experiences in the book.

News media

- Revisit the book and look again at the "newspaper" on page 24. Using the information already gathered by the Jessie and Kate groups, ask the children to write a newspaper report on their travels as it would have been written by Kate or Jessie.

Time line

- With copies of the small books for reference, the children can make a time line plotting their destinations and listing the dates on which Jessie and Kate arrived at and departed from each planet. The time line will indicate the relative distances between the planets.

- Note that the spacecraft tripled its speed between Saturn and Uranus (page 17).

Links with other Informazing books

pages 4–5	the Moon	*Small Worlds*, p. 2 *The Gas Giants*, p. 10
page 6	Venus	*Small Worlds*, pp. 4, 5, 10–11
page 7	Mercury	*Small Worlds*, pp. 4, 5, 8–9
pages 8–9	Sun	*Somewhere in the Universe*, pp. 5, 7
pages 10–11	Mars	*Small Worlds*, pp. 4, 5, 12–13
page 11	Olympus Mons	*Small Worlds*, p. 7
page 14	Jupiter	*The Gas Giants*, pp. 4–5
pages 14–15	moons	*The Gas Giants*, pp. 10–15
pages 16–17	Saturn	*The Gas Giants*, pp. 6–7
pages 18–19	Uranus	*The Gas Giants*, pp. 8–9
page 20	Neptune	*The Gas Giants*, pp. 8–9
page 21	Pluto	*Small Worlds*, pp. 4, 5, 14
page 22	comets	*Animal, Plant or Mineral?* p. 5 *The Gas Giants*, p. 8 *Small Worlds*, p. 15, 17

Compare texts: *Millions of Years Ago* shows a time line over a long period and presents the passing of time in pictorial graph form.

Investigating the night sky

- If possible, arrange a visit to an observatory or planetarium to observe the night sky, or arrange for a star-watching activity using telescopes or binoculars.

- If this is not possible, encourage children and their families to observe the night sky, and identify some of the major constellations and, at the appropriate times, planets.

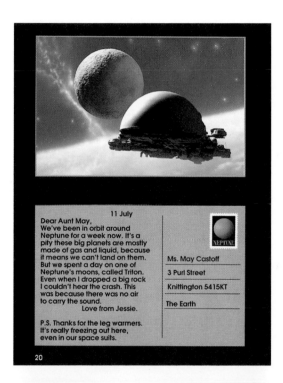

11 July

Dear Aunt May,
We've been in orbit around Neptune for a week now. It's a pity these big planets are mostly made of gas and liquid, because it means we can't land on them. But we spent a day on one of Neptune's moons, called Triton. Even when I dropped a big rock I couldn't hear the crash. This was because there was no air to carry the sound.
　　　　Love from Jessie.

P.S. Thanks for the leg warmers. It's really freezing out here, even in our space suits.

Ms. May Castoff

3 Purl Street

Knittington 5415KT

The Earth

20

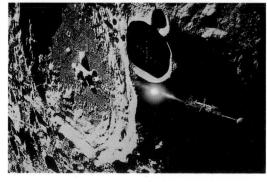

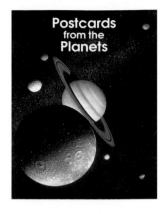

Postcards from the Planets

Left. Look closely at the pictures in the book. Some are photographs of real places such as the Sun (pages 8-9), some are paintings (page 11), and some combine photographs of model spacecraft with artwork (page 20) or with photographs of real places (page 5). Other pictures are photographs of specially built "props" as in a movie set (pages 4 and 13). Still others are collages of several photographs (page 21).

Opposite page.

A table comparing the characterization of Jessie and Kate can be made after a close reading of the text. Although this is an information book, the facts are presented as a narrative in which characterization plays a part.

Small Worlds *and* The Gas Giants

These two books provide information about the planets in the Solar System. Small Worlds looks at the four planets which are smaller than the Earth, and The Gas Giants at the four which are larger. The two books complement each other, and are treated together here for that reason.

Teacher information

• These books present information in many graphic and text styles, so the children will need time to discuss the differences and experiment with using the diagrams, cross sections, maps, etc.

> **Compare texts:** Consult *Body Maps, Skeletons, Hidden Animals*, and other Informazing books for further examples of graphic representation.

• The children will need plenty of opportunities with the small books for browsing, discussing, and examining the detail. These books also give the children opportunities to share their knowledge of planets and outer space. Children can also take them home to share with their families.

The diagram on page 3 of *Small Worlds* (**below**) was used as the reference for making models of the planets using familiar objects (**right**). This activity gives the children a clearer idea of the relative sizes of the planets.

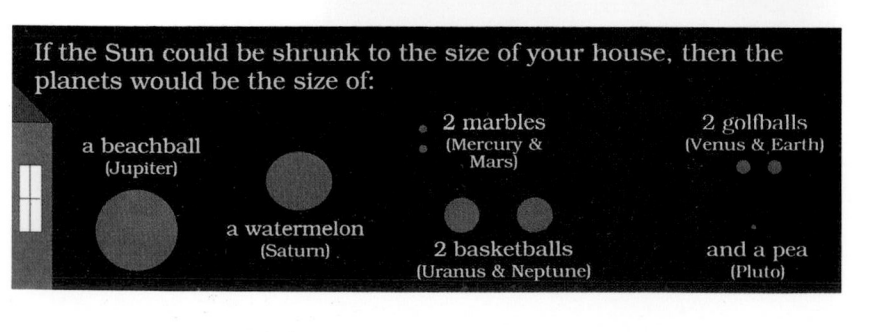

If the Sun could be shrunk to the size of your house, then the planets would be the size of:

a beachball (Jupiter)

a watermelon (Saturn)

2 basketballs (Uranus & Neptune)

2 marbles (Mercury & Mars)

2 golfballs (Venus & Earth)

and a pea (Pluto)

Features of the books

Small Worlds	The Gas Giants
Text style • Reference book format • Expository style	**Text style** • Reference book format • Expository style
Text features • Glossary • Index • Charts • Tables • Supporting information for diagrams, charts, etc. • Question and answer • Weather reports • Captions • Boxed and highlighted information	**Text features** • Glossary • Index • Supporting information for diagrams, charts, etc. • Tables • Question and answer • Captions • Boxed and highlighted information
Graphic features • Photographs • Radar map (page 11) • Size comparison charts • Cross sections • Block diagram (page 13) • Thermometer diagram (page 6) • Sequential diagrams (pages 8–9) • Artists' impressions	**Graphic features** • Size comparison charts • Cross sections • Drawings • Labelled diagrams • Photographs • Artists' impressions

You may need

• big books
• small books
• telescope
• thermometer
• hotplate or microwave oven and saucepan
• freezer or vacuum flask with ice

Introducing the books

Predicting

• Show the children the front covers and ask them what they think the books will be about.

Also ask how they think the information may be presented.

Children could sketch a rough layout of what the pages might look like, showing where their text and illustrations would be, and explain their page layouts to others. These layouts could be displayed for discussion while reading the books.

> **Teaching hint:** Even young children know a surprising amount about space and the planets. Record some of the more pertinent information on a chart for future reference. Record also the things the children would like to know for investigation later.

- Show the children the contents page establishing that each book deals with a specific number of planets.
- Give the children small copies of the books and provide time to explore them.

Examining graphics and text

- In pairs or in groups the children list the various ways in which the information has been presented. These could be categorized as graphics and text, or "illustrations" and "writing." For example:

Graphics (Illustrations)	
tables	charts
drawings	computer map
cross sections	scale drawings
labelled diagrams	photographs
maps	

Text (Writing)	
contents page	glossary
index	main paragraph
tables	related facts
supporting information	

- The children report their findings orally. These can be listed and classified for future reference. Conclude with a discussion on the specific ways in which reference books are constructed.

Representing the Solar System

- Read page 3 of *Small Worlds* (concerning the sizes and distances of the planets), and find items to represent the sizes of the planets. Take the children onto the playground or sports area, and measure 200 m (600 feet) to represent the distance from the Sun to Mercury. Imagine the other distances, and discuss where the other planets would be located.

Io

Jupiter rising behind its moon Io. The volcanoes of Io are all close together, near the equator. Some are cone-shaped while others have collapsed to become holes in the ground where the sulfur oozes out

Moon of volcanoes

Io is the only moon that is known for certain to have active volcanoes. Instead of lava the volcanoes produce a poisonous gas called sulfur. Io has 8 volcanoes.

The polar mountains Near the north and south poles of Io are mountains that are higher than the Himalayas. They are 10 kilometres high.

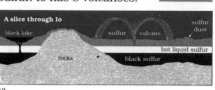

A slice through Io

black lake · sulfur · volcano · sulfur dust · hot liquid sulfur · rocks · black sulfur

12

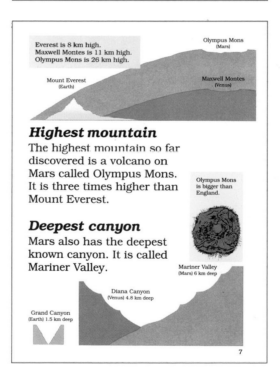

Everest is 8 km high.
Maxwell Montes is 11 km high.
Olympus Mons is 26 km high.

Olympus Mons (Mars)

Mount Everest (Earth)

Maxwell Montes (Venus)

Highest mountain

The highest mountain so far discovered is a volcano on Mars called Olympus Mons. It is three times higher than Mount Everest.

Olympus Mons is bigger than England.

Deepest canyon

Mars also has the deepest known canyon. It is called Mariner Valley.

Mariner Valley (Mars) 6 km deep

Diana Canyon (Venus) 4.8 km deep

Grand Canyon (Earth) 1.5 km deep

7

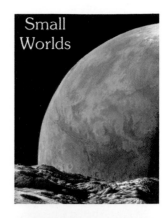

Small Worlds

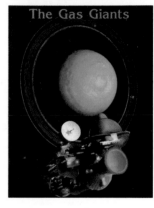

The Gas Giants

Both these books use a variety of graphic features, such as silhouette diagrams and maps (**left**) as well as airbrush paintings, labelled diagrams and cross sections (**above left**).

Today's Weather

May 16

	Mars	Mercury	Venus
Temperature	Below freezing	So hot you would burn up.	Boiling.
Wind	Strong winds. Dust storms.	—	Hurricanes
Moisture	—	—	Acid rain.
Cloud	Light cloud, morning fogs.	—	THICK CLOUDS ALL DAY.
Other	Expanding ice caps.	Starry sky all day!	Lightning

Top. Children can summarize the weather data in *Small Worlds* by arranging the information as a table.

Above. Working together the children design and fill in another table comparing the main features of two of the planets.

Investigating days and years

- A day on Venus lasts eight months, and a year on Mercury lasts three months (*Small Worlds*, page 6). Discuss with the children what this means, and how it happens.

- The children can investigate, and make a table of, the lengths of the day and of the year on each planet. Examples of similar tables are given in *Small Worlds* (page 4) and *The Gas Giants* (page 3).

- Children can make dioramas of the surface of a planet using the pictures in *Small Worlds* as reference.

Weather

- Research weather records on Earth. For example:
  - highest temperature: in the world, in your country, or in your town;
  - lowest temperature: in the world, in your country, in your town;
  - wettest, hottest, driest place or day;
  - longest period of rain or drought;
  - which countries get the most snow, rain, sun, droughts, floods, etc.

The Guinness Book of Records and your local weather office are useful resources for this activity.

- Invite a meteorologist to answer the children's questions. Ensure that the children have prepared pertinent questions and done some research first.

- Record one or two weather forecasts from the radio or TV for the children to hear. Discuss the style, tone and presentation of the language. Ask them to bring weather forecasts cut out of the paper. Display these for comment.

- Ask the children, working in pairs with the small books, to read the weather forecasts in *Small Worlds* (pages 9, 11, 12) to each other. When they have finished, ask the children to write a weather forecast for each planet in *The Gas Giants*. Children will need to consult the text closely to complete the task.

- The children now present their written forecast as a radio or TV broadcast. Display their written work and discuss the differences in style, tone, and vocabulary between the written and the spoken forecasts.

Drawing cross sections

- The children find something which they can cut to make a cross section, for example fruit, vegetables, or pieces of wood. When cut in different ways all of these show different patterns.

- In small groups, the children can cut, draw, and label the items.
- In pairs with the small books, children can study the cross-section drawings in the small books, and read the appropriate text. For example,
  - *Small Worlds*, page 13.
  - *The Gas Giants*, pages 4, 5, 9, 12, 13.

> **Compare texts:** *Body Maps*, pages 9, 10–11, 12, and 13 also show cross sections.

The "greenhouse planet"

- In *Small Worlds* Venus is described as the "greenhouse planet." Revisit the book (pages 10–11), asking the children to note the important features of Venus.

> **Compare texts:** *Postcards from the Planets* (page 6) tells of the spacecraft's stop near Venus. *Earth in Danger* explains global warming (pages 10–11), which is also known as the "greenhouse effect."

Make sure that the children are aware of what a greenhouse (or glasshouse) is and what it does. The effect is similar to the inside of a car on a hot day in the sun with all the windows closed.

- From the class notes, which should be clearly displayed, the children could draw pictures of what they think a Venus landscape looks like.

Investigating scientific concepts

Many scientific ideas are presented in these two books. The following activities explore and extend some of these ideas.

Temperature

- Ask the children to bring from home thermometers of different kinds. Discuss the purposes for which these are used, the ways in which they differ, and the range in temperature each measures. For example:
  - a doctor's thermometer accurately measures body temperature but has only a tiny range from about 34° to 44°C (90° to 110°F);
  - a thermometer to measure air temperature has a much wider range, but is less accurate.
- Keep a record of the classroom and playground temperatures over a month.
- Using the freezing compartment of a refrigerator and a frypan or oven, measure

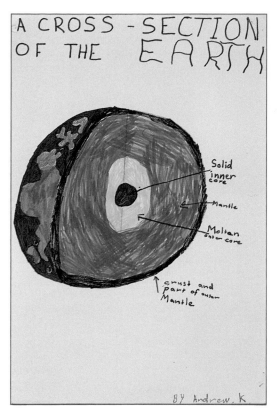

A CROSS-SECTION OF THE EARTH

Solid inner core
Mantle
Molten outer core
crust and part of outer Mantle

BY Andrew. K.

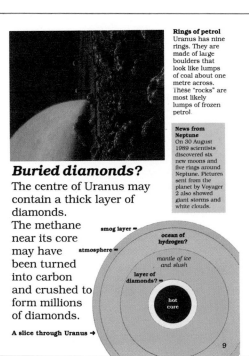

Rings of petrol
Uranus has nine rings. They are made of large boulders that look like lumps of coal about one metre across. These "rocks" are most likely lumps of frozen petrol.

News from Neptune
On 30 August 1989 scientists discovered six new moons and five rings around Neptune. Pictures sent from the planet by Voyager 2 also showed giant storms and white clouds.

Buried diamonds?
The centre of Uranus may contain a thick layer of diamonds. The methane near its core may have been turned into carbon and crushed to form millions of diamonds.

A slice through Uranus →

smog layer
atmosphere
ocean of hydrogen?
mantle of ice and slush
layer of diamonds?
hot core

9

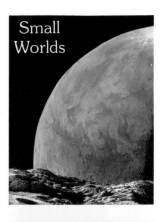

Small Worlds

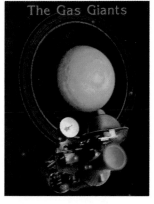

The Gas Giants

After studying the cross section diagrams in *The Gas Giants* (**left**) Andrew produced a cross section of the Earth (**above left**) for which he needed to refer to additional books.

Mars

The red planet
Red desert sands and rocks give Mars its colour.

Weather report

Summer
The melting ice caps will cause increasing cloud, but no rain. Early morning fogs. Strong winds and dust storms are expected to last for four months. Temperatures will be around 10° below freezing — on the hottest days.

Winter
Temperatures will fall to around 100° below freezing and the ice caps will grow larger. Calm days with clear skies.

Is there life on Mars?

Mars is a planet of icy deserts. Space craft that have landed on Mars have found no life there. Living things need water, but all the water on Mars is frozen.

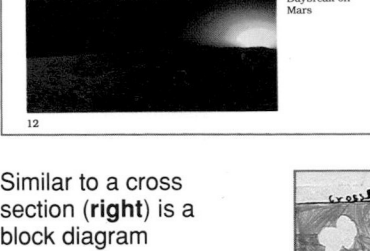

Daybreak on Mars

Rivers on Mars
In the past the ice on Mars melted and flowed as rivers. These rivers may have lasted only a few weeks before the water froze again. Volcanoes probably caused the ice to melt. Now the river valleys are dry — even though they are sometimes filled with mist.

Voyage to Mars

The first astronauts to visit Mars are expected to arrive sometime about the year 2020. The round trip (including exploration of Mars) will last about three years.

A slice through Mars

desert — sand dune — canyon — ice cap

volcano — frozen soil

12   13

Similar to a cross section (**right**) is a block diagram (**above**) which shows the landscape features of Mars.
Other graphic features of *Small Worlds* are photographs, artists' impressions, and radar maps (**below**).

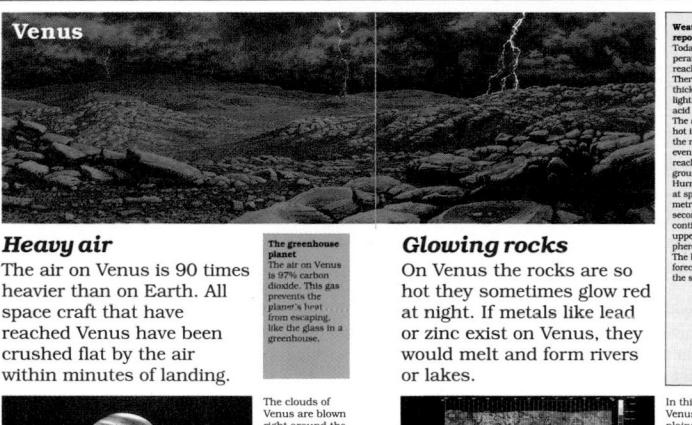

Venus

Heavy air

The air on Venus is 90 times heavier than on Earth. All space craft that have reached Venus have been crushed flat by the air within minutes of landing.

The greenhouse planet
The air on Venus is 97% carbon dioxide. This gas prevents the planet's heat from escaping, like the glass in a greenhouse.

Glowing rocks

On Venus the rocks are so hot they sometimes glow red at night. If metals like lead or zinc exist on Venus, they would melt and form rivers or lakes.

Weather report
Today the temperature will reach 460°C. There will be thick cloud, lightning and acid rain. The air will be so hot it will turn the rain to steam even before it reaches the ground. Hurricane winds at speeds of 100 metres per second will continue in the upper atmosphere. The long range forecast: more of the same.

The clouds of Venus are blown right around the planet once every four days. Although the planet is hot, its clouds are freezing cold.

In this map of Venus, lowland plains are blue and highlands are red or yellow. There are no oceans or seas.

10   11

---

extremes of temperature with a thermometer. *Warning*: for the frypan experiment, check first that the range of the thermometer used (such as an oven thermometer) reaches 300°C (600°F). An adult must be present.

These activities will help children to appreciate more fully the temperatures on the planets, besides providing a meaningful context for using thermometers.

Teaching hint: Some children may be interested in the extremes of temperature that are possible. The temperature on Pluto is −270°C (−450°F) at night. Explain to the children that this is close to "absolute zero" (−273°C). This means that it is very nearly as cold as it is possible to be. There is no "absolute maximum"—the temperature of the Sun is 15 million degrees and other stars are hotter.

Gases, liquids, and solids

● Discuss what happens to substances as the temperature goes up or down. Children will be familiar with water boiling and freezing. Ask about other substances, which change states at higher or lower temperatures. For example, butter will turn to liquid on a hot day.

● Demonstrate evaporation. Stand a glass of water in direct sunlight on a hot day. Each hour, measure the height of the water. It's disappearing! Where is the water when the glass is empty? For comparison set up a second glass of water in a cooler part of the room.

● Set two glasses of water in the hot sun. Cover one with black paper or paint it black. Put a thermometer in each glass. Check that they are initially at the same temperature. Measure and record the temperature every five minutes. Try a third glass covered with foil. Why are there differences?

Experiments at high temperatures cannot be undertaken in the classroom. However, children may have seen a lava flow or a steelworks on TV, and could relate the "glowing rocks" on Venus (*Small Worlds*, page 11) to the flowing lava or the glowing metal at a steelworks.

● Children can investigate the temperatures at which metals and other substances change from solid to liquid, and make a table, or use the model of the thermometer on page 6 of *Small Worlds*, to show their findings.

Geology

- These two books also raise questions on the formation of landscapes. Page 8 of *Small Worlds* shows the formation of a crater. Discuss the ways in which our landforms on Earth have evolved, for example through volcanic action, earthquakes, and erosion by wind and water. There may be features in your local landscape which will provide examples that can be visited and discussed.

- To simulate the formation of a crater, watch what happens when you throw a rock into a sandpit and then into a still pool of water; finally throw a rock into a tub of fresh dough.

Experiments with color

- Discuss why the sky is a different color on different planets. What different colors do we see in the sky on Earth, for example, in the morning or evening, and at night?

- Show the colors in the light we receive from the Sun by setting up a glass of water on a windowsill. Observe the rainbow (spectrum) formed on a sheet of paper next to the glass. Look at the spectrum on the paper through a magnifying glass, and name the colors. Finally place colored cellophane over the glass. Do some or all of the colors disappear from the spectrum?

The effect of smog

- Read "The smog planets" on page 8 of *The Gas Giants*. What causes smog on Earth?

- Are there any lichens growing near your school? Lichens are the first plants to die if smog is present. Go out and investigate.

Links with other Informazing books

All the planets are mentioned in *Postcards from the Planets*. Other links are:

Small Worlds		
page 16	ozone layer	*Earth in Danger*, pp. 14, 15

The Gas Giants		
page 8	smog	*Earth in Danger*, p. 3
page 16	"4000 million years ago"	*Millions of Years Ago* (time lines)

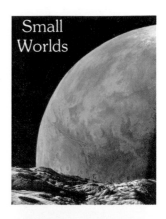

The sequential diagram "How craters are made" (**below left**) was used as the basis for experimenting with materials (**left**). Different substances (sand, water, wet plaster, and cement) were bombarded with pebbles and the "craters" compared.

The giant crater

Mercury is the planet with the largest crater, called the Caloris Basin.

It is the size of western Europe.

Mercury is covered with craters that were formed when lumps of rock called meteors crashed into the planet more than 3000 million years ago.

The Caloris meteor sent shock waves through Mercury and pushed up mountains on the far side of the planet. The mountains are 2000 metres high and were formed in less than 10 minutes.

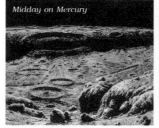
Midday on Mercury

A planet that shrank

Mercury is the only planet that is thought to have shrunk. The shrinking of Mercury forced rocks to the surface that formed giant cliffs 3 km high.

Weather report
Today's temperature will reach 430° C, but will fall by 600° overnight. Because there is no air, there will be no wind and no clouds. The stars will shine all day. Tomorrow's weather will be exactly the same.

The fastest planet
Mercury is the fastest moving planet. It travels at 48 km per second.

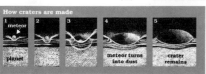
How craters are made
1 meteor 2 3 4 meteor turns into dust 5 crater remains
planet

At first Mercury expanded, causing deep cracks in its surface.

Later the planet shrank, forcing rocks up through the cracks.

8   9

Earth in Danger

Earth in Danger examines the reasons for the Earth's climatic changes and raises contemporary issues related to environmental studies. This book is a springboard for the investigation of many issues. Scientific concepts and understandings can be developed in the context of the environment.

Features of the book

Text style	Graphic features
● Information	● Labelled drawings
	● Diagrams
Text features	● Maps
● Contents	● Graphs
● Index	● Photographs
● Glossary	● Flow charts
● Bibliography	● Computer graphics (page 14)

You may need

- big book
- small books
- world climate maps
- daily weather reports and weather maps
- thermometer

The issues presented in this book are both topical and controversial. The children will have much to offer. List the information which they put forward on a large sheet of paper. This may be used as a source for looking at fact and opinion, as well as for stimulating further investigations.

Introducing the book

Alternative 1:
Predicting

● Cover the title and ask the children in small groups to write a few lines about the photograph on the front cover. Share and display these.

In one grade 5 and 6 class, the children's responses to the cover photograph were:

The picture makes us feel as though we are really in the forest right next to the waterfall. It is a lush green forest and looks as though it has lots of beautiful birds and animals in it. The trees look as if they are very big. In nature's way it makes the forest beautiful.

● Move to page 1 (the title page), still concealing the title, and ask the children again to write a few lines about the photographs.

● Ask the children to discuss and to predict what they think the book will be about. List their responses to compare with the text.

In the same grade 5 and 6 class, the children's responses to the pictures on the title page were:

I think the book is about nature. It shows pollution, soil erosion, power, and logging.

Big chimneys are polluting the world with all the smoke coming out of them. This picture reminds us of logging and where it's sand is where they've cut the trees down.

● Read the book with the children, referring to their predictions.

Alternative 2:
Interpreting photographs

Teaching hint: Cover the lower photograph and the text on pages 12–13 including the captions for the illustrations, leaving only the top two photographs showing.

● Ask the children to write a newspaper article based on the two photographs on pages 12–13. The children can compare texts and explain the points they have made.

● Read the text on pages 12–13. Discuss the impact of the photographs in getting messages across.

● Read the book with the children, allowing time for comment, particularly on the relation of the text to the photographs.

These approaches to the book indicate the importance of visual information in society.

Pictures are used for the purpose of:

- selling
- persuasion
- education
- information

Constructing questions

● In small groups and using the small books, the children list questions related to the topics raised in the book.

● Display these and compare what different groups have written.

● As a class, sort the questions into categories under headings such as:

Information	How to change?	Issues

and make a set of agreed questions. These can form the basis for research, or perhaps for writing away for further information.

The same grade 5 and 6 class made this list:

Information	How to change?	Issues
Can we use solar power for cars?	What about using string bags instead of plastic?	If the loggers care about the Earth, why do they cut down the trees?
How big do the holes in the ozone layer get every day?	What other things can we do to save the Earth?	Why doesn't the government do anything about the environment?
Which are the countries most in danger?	Why can't the government get rid of all the CFC spray cans?	Why are people careless and thoughtless?
How many trees are cut down each day?	How can we use less writing paper at school?	
How long does it take for the ozone layer to heal?	Can we use a waterwheel to generate power?	

Teaching hint: As children begin their research, they will find they need to modify some of their questions. For instance, they will discover that the size of ozone holes cannot be monitored daily.

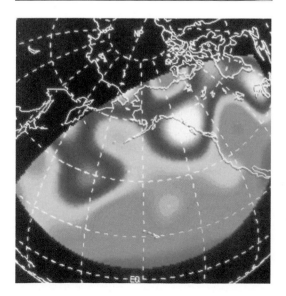

> The children showed great awareness of environmental issues in constructing questions, but also confusion between the different kinds of environmental hazards. For example, they confused the hole in the ozone layer with the greenhouse effect, and thought leaded gasoline contributed to the damage in the ozone layer. This book provided the stimulus for investigating and clarifying these concepts, as well as looking at ways of solving some of the problems.
> —*Grade 5-6 teacher*

Left. Ask the children to predict what the book will be about, as indicated by the photographs on page 1.

Below left. A computer-generated map shows ozone holes (white areas) passing over North America.

Below. Compare the three pictures on pages 2-3. Children write captions for page 2 using the caption on page 3 as a model.

Earth in danger
Planet Earth is in danger. The climate is heating up, which may cause seas to rise and flood our cities. We pour our waste into the rivers and the skies. Some farms are turning into deserts. Forests are being destroyed and many animals and plants are disappearing. What has caused these changes and what can we do about it?

3

The future   113

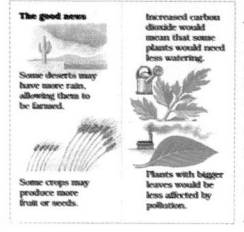

If the world gets warmer
What would happen if the world became warmer? A warm climate would make some rivers dry up while others would flood. Hurricanes could strike cities such as Washington, Rome and Sydney which have not been hit by hurricanes

(or tropical cyclones) before. Warmer oceans would have less oxygen which fish depend on. Crops would fail in parts of the USA and Australia. On the other hand, crops could be grown in parts of northern Canada, Siberia and Scotland that are now too cold for growing crops.

8   9

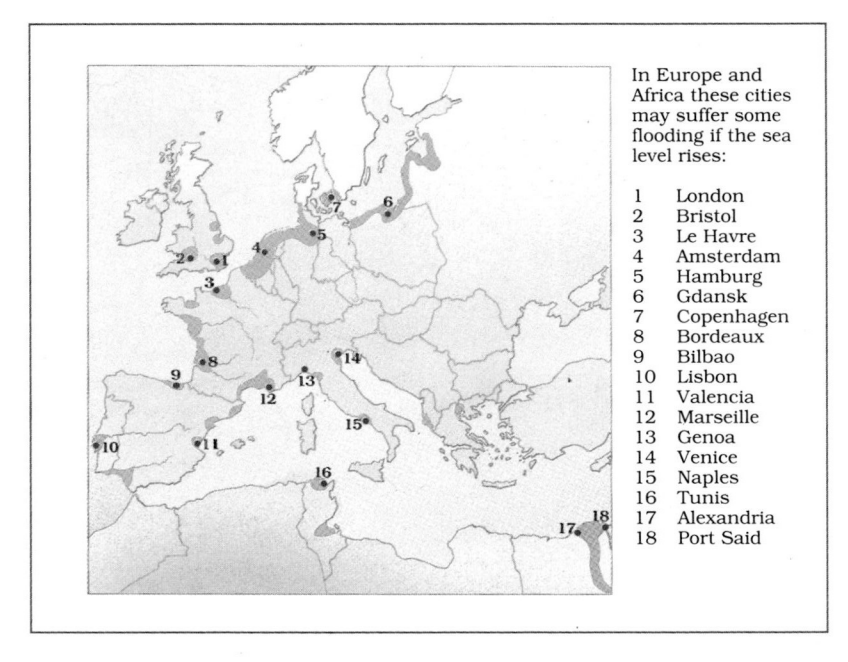

In Europe and Africa these cities may suffer some flooding if the sea level rises:

1   London
2   Bristol
3   Le Havre
4   Amsterdam
5   Hamburg
6   Gdansk
7   Copenhagen
8   Bordeaux
9   Bilbao
10 Lisbon
11 Valencia
12 Marseille
13 Genoa
14 Venice
15 Naples
16 Tunis
17 Alexandria
18 Port Said

Ask the children to write a news report based on the labelled diagram (**top**) and the map of Europe (**above**).

Areas for investigation

● Each page of this book provides a topic for investigation and an issue for debate. If children have constructed questions, these can be used as the basis for research.

Global warming (the "greenhouse effect")

Graphing

● Pages 10–11 present information about "global warming" gases. The strip graphs ("What makes carbon dioxide?" etc.) each add up to 100% and can be redrawn as pie charts. The children can transfer the information in the strip graphs to bar or pie graphs.

Making a terrarium

● The children can make a terrarium with a large plastic bottle cut off at the neck, a large glass container, a glass aquarium, or a sheet of clear plastic. Fill a waterproof base with damp potting mix and plant it with small plants. Cover the base with the inverted bottle or the plastic.

● Over a period of time, observe what happens. The children can discuss their observations, and present these in diagrams.

> The terrarium is a closed system, and can be considered a model of the ecology of the rainforest. The canopy of the rainforest creates a microclimate, as does the enclosed terrarium.

Recommending action

● Ask the children to discuss and write recommendations for action based on the information on pages 10–11. Their recommendations could be presented in the form of an advertising poster.

Maps

● The maps on pages 6–7 show coastal areas which may in the future be in danger of flooding. The children can identify these areas on a globe or world map, such as the map on page 18.

Newspapers

● The children can collect newspaper articles related to the issues raised in *Earth in Danger*.

> Collecting relevant newspaper articles could be an alternative introduction to this topic.

These articles can be used both to provide further information and to raise issues for discussion.

Climate

• Ask the children to estimate the temperature at the present moment. Check this, both inside and outside, with a thermometer.

• Ask the children to estimate the average maximum and minimum temperatures for their area. Check these in an atlas or encyclopedia.

• The children can also estimate, and then check, the average yearly rainfall for their area. Compare this with the rainfall in other areas which the children know.

• The children can investigate and report on other theories about climate besides those presented in *Earth in Danger*.

Recycling

• The children can investigate recycling, how it is done in their local area, and how it could be improved.

Debate or role play

• The children can identify an issue from the book, and debate or role-play possible actions to take. For example, from the photograph on page 3 they might identify public versus private transportation as an issue. They could then take the parts of a local resident wishing to improve public transportation and a worker at a car factory wanting the factory enlarged, to persuade a politician of their points of view.

The local area

• The children can identify conservation issues within their local area, for example drift-net fishing, deforestation or acid rain. They can research the issue, and make recommendations for some action that they could take personally to contribute to solving the problem. They could also recommend actions that need to be taken at the community, local government, or state government level. The worksheet "Save the Earth" (page 132 below) can be used to complete this activity.

Links with other Informazing books

| pages 10–11 | greenhouse effect | *Small Worlds*, p. 10 |

Left. A special flap at the back of the book folds out so that the map and glossary can be consulted as the text of the rest of the book is being read.

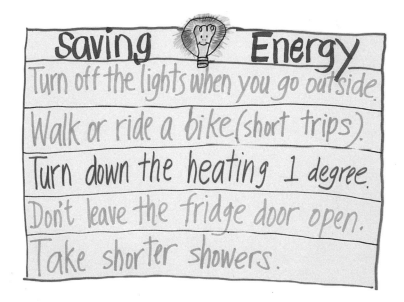

Above. How can we do something positive to save energy? Children can make a chart and select items for personal or community action.

I'm in Danger

Name

I have ☐ legs, ☐ wings, ☐ tail, ☐ ....

Description:

Picture:

I'm in danger because

I live in the

I need   in order to survive.

You can help me by

119

Before and After

I drew a

It looked like

Under the microscope it looked like this:

Write about the differences.

_____

_____

_____

_____

My Hidden Animal

When my animal is camouflaged it looks like this:

Here is my animal:

Label the parts of your animal.

My animal lives in the

My animal is a

World Map

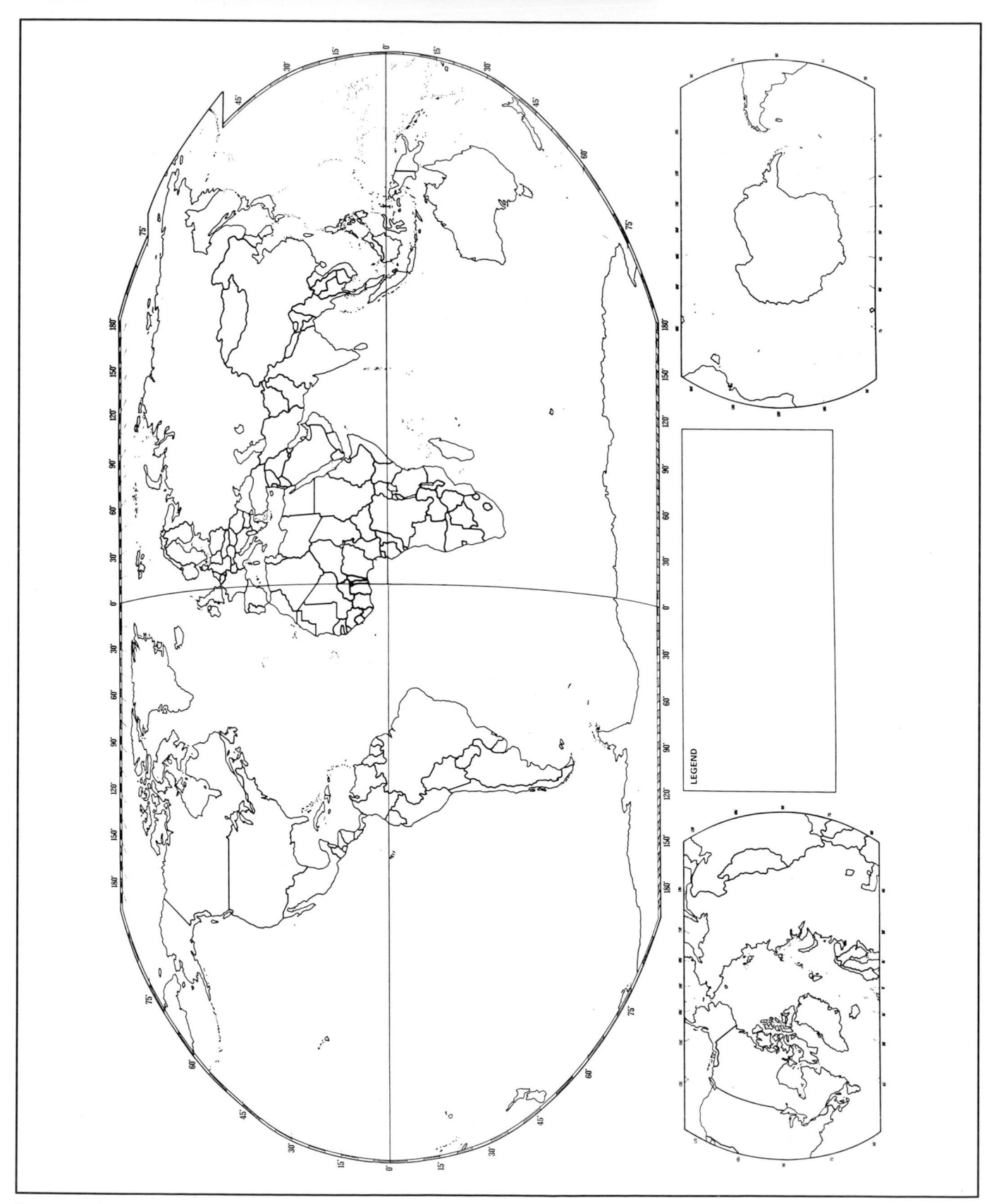

LEGEND

Animal Symmetry

crab

grasshopper

butterfly

sea star

Draw the line of symmetry for each animal.
Color each animal to show symmetrical patterns.

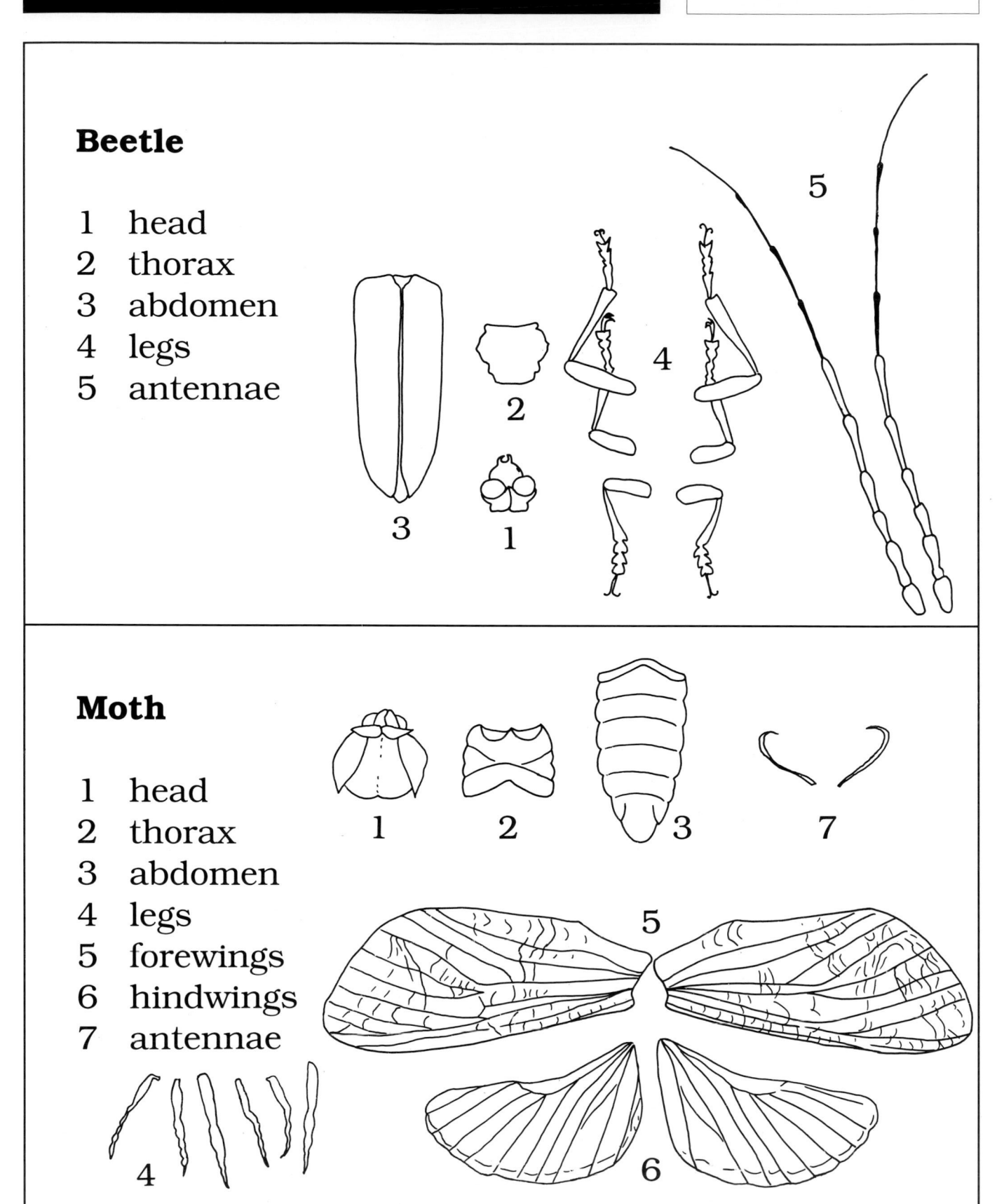

Beetle

1 head
2 thorax
3 abdomen
4 legs
5 antennae

Moth

1 head
2 thorax
3 abdomen
4 legs
5 forewings
6 hindwings
7 antennae

My Pet's Food

My pet is a

_____

My pet eats

_____

_____

_____

My pet is fed
at these times:

(12) _____

(12) _____

My pet eats this much
food at each meal:

Heights and Jumps

First estimate, then measure your height.

I estimate I am _____ tall.

My measured height is _____ .

Estimate how far you can jump.
Then jump and measure the distance.

Standing Jump

I think I can jump _____ .

In fact I jumped _____ .

Running Start

I think I can jump _____ .

In fact I jumped _____ .

Animal Facts

Name	Habitat
Size ├──────────┤ scale	**Food**
Enemies	**Mystery Fact**

127

Tadpole Diary

Week

Now our tadpoles look like this:

This is how they have changed:

Things our tadpoles can do:

Pulse and Breathing

Measure your pulse and breathing rates before and after exercise.

Before running around the block:

    my pulse rate was _____ beats per minute.
    my breathing rate was _____ breaths per minute.

After running around the block:

    my pulse rate was _____ beats per minute.
    my breathing rate was _____ breaths per minute.

Present your findings as a graph.
Ask a friend to interpret it.

129

Southern Stars

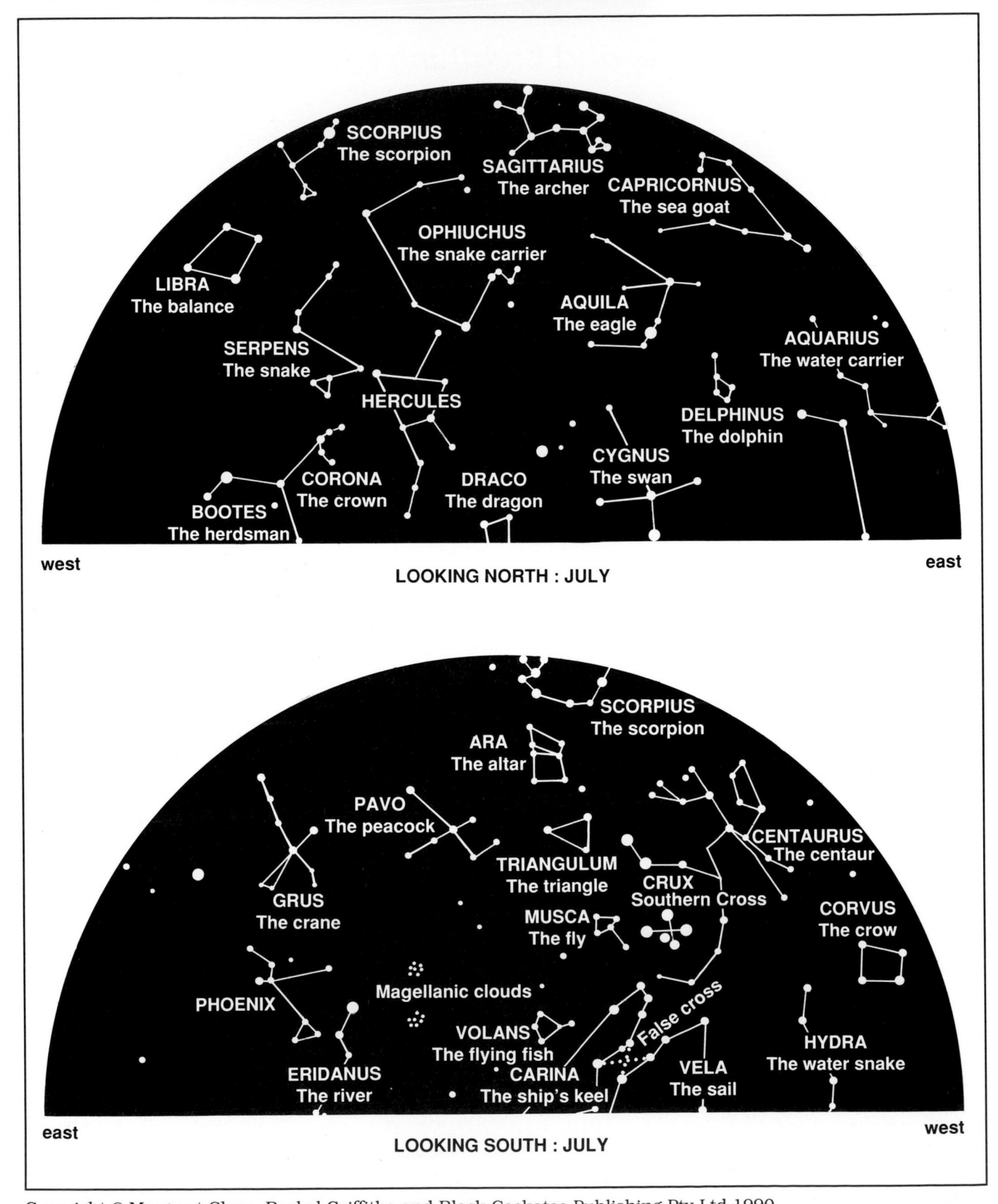

SCORPIUS
The scorpion

SAGITTARIUS
The archer

CAPRICORNUS
The sea goat

OPHIUCHUS
The snake carrier

LIBRA
The balance

AQUILA
The eagle

AQUARIUS
The water carrier

SERPENS
The snake

HERCULES

DELPHINUS
The dolphin

CORONA
The crown

DRACO
The dragon

CYGNUS
The swan

BOOTES
The herdsman

west

east

LOOKING NORTH : JULY

SCORPIUS
The scorpion

ARA
The altar

PAVO
The peacock

TRIANGULUM
The triangle

CRUX
Southern Cross

CENTAURUS
The centaur

GRUS
The crane

MUSCA
The fly

CORVUS
The crow

Magellanic clouds

PHOENIX

VOLANS
The flying fish

False cross

HYDRA
The water snake

ERIDANUS
The river

CARINA
The ship's keel

VELA
The sail

east

west

LOOKING SOUTH : JULY

Northern Stars

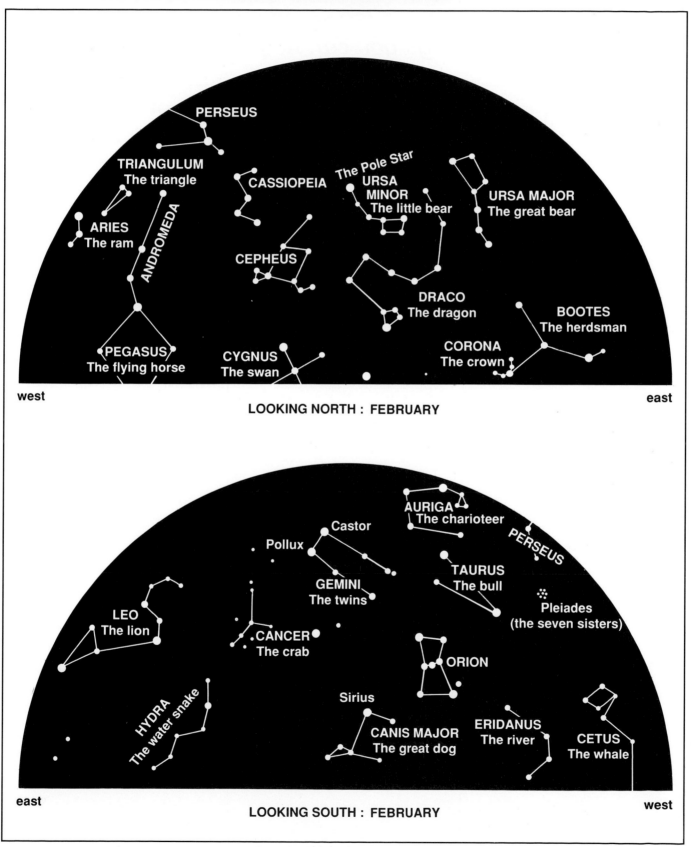

LOOKING NORTH : FEBRUARY

LOOKING SOUTH : FEBRUARY

131

Save the Earth

List some of the ways you can help protect the planet.		
The problem	Actions I can take	Actions the community can take
The "greenhouse effect"		
Rainforest clearing		
Ozone holes		
Air pollution		
Water pollution		
Acid rain		

Index

Part 4

Entries in italics (such as *21*) refer to illustrations.
Entries in bold type (such as **21**) are main entries.

a

abbreviations, lists of, 58
acid rain, 115
addresses, 102, *103*
aerial views, *101*
airbrush paintings, *107*
alphabetical order, 28, 47, *54*
amphibians, *31*, 78–81
Animal Acrobats, 37, 40, 41, 45, 49, 52, 61, **66-69**, 81, 84, 85, 93
Animal Clues, 20, 22, 24, 28, 37, 40, 41, **46-49**, 51, 52, 57, 61, 65, 69, 73, 81, 93, 97
Animal, Plant or Mineral? 21, 22, 24, 25, 35, 37, 41, 52, 57, 61, 65, 73, 77, 85, 89, **90-93**, 97, 105
animals, 90–93
animals, diet of, 62–65
animals, distribution of, 42
animals, endangered, 32–33
animals, extinct, 32–33
animals, eyesight of, **54-57**
animals, food for, *73*
animals, mating, *73*
animals, movement of, **66-69**, *80*
animals, nocturnal, *52*
animals, observed in classroom, 70–81, *77*
animals, parts of, 51
animals, prehistoric, **30-33**
art, *105*
"artist's impressions," 86, 106, *110*
arts and crafts, **24**, *25*
assessment, *see* "evaluation"
astronauts, 103
atlas conventions, *100*, 101
atom, *89*

b

bacteria, *88, 89*
bar graphs, 62, *63, 65*
bears, *65*
bibliographies, 112
big books, 10, 26, 31
big books, as stimulus for research, 113
big books, as writing models, 17, 24, 48, *51, 56*, 60
big books, can be read backwards, 98
big books, comparing fact and fiction in, 102
big books, concealing the text of, *38*, 46, 90–91, *92*
big books, need not be read in full, 62
big books, not read through on first reading, 34
big books, shared with only half the class, 35, 39
birds, 43, 44, *67, 69, 80*
"bird's eye view," 100, *101*
block diagrams, 106, *110*
blood, *87, 88*
blurbs, 34, 38, 54, 82, *94, 98*, 102
board games, 21, 34, 37, 78, 81
Body Facts, 26, 30, 47, 57, 85, **86-89**, 92, 93, 97
Body Maps, 21, 24, 42, 43, 57, 61, 69, **82-85**, 86, 87, 89, 92, 93, 95, 97, 101, 106, 109
body parts, 57, 68, *69*, 75, *80*, **82-89**, *83, 124*
bones, 42–45, **82-89**
Book of Animal Records, The, 21, 32, 33, 41, 45, 49, 55, 56, 57, **58-61**, 65, 68, 69, 81, 87, 93
boxed text, 82, 86, *87*, 90, *94*, 106
brain, 85

breathing, 87, *88*
butterflies, 70–73
butterfly, eggs of, *95*

c

calendars, 30, 62, 63, 65
camera, pinhole, 56
camouflage, 36, **38-41**
captions, 20, 21, 34, 66, 82–85, 86, 106, 113
carnivores, 64
catalogues, library, 26, 102
Caterpillar Diary, 37, 41, 52, 57, 72, 73, **74-77**, 81, 89, 93, 97, 103
Caterpillar Diary frieze, 11, **74-75**
caterpillars, 70–71, 73, **74-77**, *91*
cells, 87, *89*
chameleons, *69*
characterization, *104–105*
charts, 32, 39, 48, *84*, 98, 106, *115, see also* "lists," "tables"
charts, flow, *63*, 66, 78, *80*, *112*
charts, illustrated, 58
charts, pie, 74, 80
classification of library books, 97, 102
classification, informal, 43
classification, scientific, 45
classifying, 24
classifying animals, 36, 41, 43, **44-45**, 48, 50, 52, 66, 76
classifying foods, 62–65
classifying living things, 90–93
classifying materials, 90–93
classroom organization, **27-28**
climate, 108, 115
clock faces, 62
collaborative reading, 35, 39, 42, 54
color coding, 21, 30, 34, 58, 70, 74, 78, 82, 83, 84, 85
color coding, on diagrams, 74
color coding, on maps, 101
color, *97*, 111
color-coded text, 90
colored text, 98
column graphs, 62
comet dust, *92*
comprehension, 26
computer graphics, 86, 112
concealing the text, as an aid to discussion, *38*, 40, 46, 80, 90–91, *92*
conservation, *112–115*
constellations, 98, *130, 131*
contents page, compared with index, 66
contents page, use of, 107
contents pages, 20, 21, 33, 58, 66, 70, 74, 76, 78, 82, 86, 87, 99, 107, 112
contents pages, comparing, 76
counting, *19*, 25, *53*
countries, 99
crabs, *48*
craters, 111
Creature Features, *19*, 37, 41, 49, **50-53**, 57, 69, 73, 75, 93, 97
cross references, 20, 34, 36
cross sections, 17, 20, *28*, 30, 66, 82, 84, 85, 95, 106, *107*, 108, *109, 110*
crystals, 97

d

days and years, 108
debating issues, 23, 33, 114, 115
deforestation, 115
diagrams, 106
diagrams, as reference, *106*
diagrams, block, 106, *110*
diagrams, color coding on, 74
diagrams, compared with photographs, *66, 67*
diagrams, distortion in, 82
diagrams, enlargement, 82
diagrams, exploded, 82
diagrams, food web, *27, 40*
diagrams, labelled, 20, 23, 38, 58, *59*, 66, *69*, 75, 78, *80*, 82, 86, 106, 112, *114*
diagrams, life cycle, *28, 76*
diagrams, scale, 58, 66, 68, 70, 72, *73*, 78
diagrams, sequential, 100, 106, 111
diagrams, silhouette, 30, 60, *107*
diagrams, temperature, 106
diagrams, Venn, *44, 52*
diaries, 64, 72, **74-77**, **78-81**, 103
diary, as record of observations, 75
diary, compared with expository text, 74
diary, compared with postcard, 75
diary, purposes for, 75
dictionary conventions, 41, 57
dictionary, use of, 81, 83, 71, 90
diet, 62–65
dinosaur, skull of, *23*
dinosaurs, *30*, 31
dioramas, 108
discussion, 10
discussion of pictures, 31
distortion in diagrams, 82
drafts, 51
dragonflies, *35*
drawing while observing, 23
drawings, life-size, 77, 81

e

ear, 85
Earth in Danger, 22, 26, 33, 41, 81, 109, 111, **112-115**
Earth, *109*, **112-115**
Earth, evolution of, 31
elephants, *23*
encyclopedia conventions, 41
encyclopedia, use of, 83, 90
enlargement diagrams, 82
environment, 62, *97*, **112-115**
environmental print, 98
estimating mass, 62
estimating size, 36
estimating speed, 67
estimating time, 62, 67, 77
Europe, *114*
evaluation, 22, **27-28**
evaporation, 110
evolution, 30–33
excursions, *see* "field trips"
exercise, 88
exploded diagrams, 82
expository text, 30, 58–61, 66, *73*, 78, 86, *96*, 106, 112

extinction, 32–33
eye, *88, 93, 95*
eye color, 56
eyesight, **54-57**

f

fact and fiction, 26, 102
factories, 115
facts, changing, 26
family involvement, 26–27, 105, 106
fiction, 102, *see also* "narrative"
field trips, 27
field trips to museums, 32
field trips to zoos, 39, 51, **64**
field trips, to observe animals, 78
first person narrative, 74, 79
first person text, 92
fish, *40, 69,* 81
flies, *95*
flight, *69*
flow charts, *63,* 66, 78, *80, 112*
food groups, 62–65
food web diagrams, *27, 40*
freezing point, 110
friezes, 11, **70-71**
friezes, as reference for oral reports, 73
friezes, compared with books, 74, 79
friezes, labelling of, 79
friezes, making, 33
friezes, separating text from picture in, 70
friezes, sequencing of, 71
friezes, used to evaluate prior knowledge, *70*
friezes, used to make time lines, 77
frogs, *47, 67, 69,* 78–81

g

galaxies, *99*
games, 24–26, *see also* "problems, solving"
games, as preparation for reading, 90
Gas Giants, The, 20, 22, 26, 30, 33, 81, 87, 101, 103, 105, **106-111**
gases, 110
generalizations, 17, *83*
genus, 45
geography, 99–101
geology, 111
germs, *89*
glossaries, 20, 21, 41, 57, *58,* 58–59, 69, *80,* 81, 87, 106, 112, *115*
glossary, compiling a, 81, 87
graphics and text, compared, *65,* 107
graphics, children's, 114
graphics, comparing, 106
graphics, computer-generated, 86, 112
graphs, 20, 56, 58, 60, 62
graphs, as summaries, 63
graphs, bar, 62, *63, 65*
graphs, column, 62
graphs, misleading, 63
grasshoppers, *41, 48*
gravity, 103
"greenhouse effect," 22, 23, 26, 109, 113, **114**
guessing cards, 89

h

habitats, 35, 38, 40–41, *73, 74*
hair, 84, *88*
headings, 20, 21, 34, 58, 66, 72, 74, 78
health, 62, 88, *97*
hearing, 85
herbivores, 64
Hidden Animals, 20, *27,* 33, 36, 37, **38-41,** 45, 49, 51, 52, 56, 57, 61, 65, 69, 73, 75, 77, 78, 92, 93, 97, 106
historical sequences, 33
human body, **82-89**
hygiene, 62, 63

i

I Spy, 19, 24, 25, 37, 40, 41, 45, 49, **54-57,** 69, 73, 81, 89, 93, 97
illness, 88
illustrations, 40
illustrations from different perspectives, *30–31,* 98
illustrations, comparing, 42
illustrations, labelled, 30, 62, 98
illustrations, used to predict the text, 107
impersonal tone, 17, *83, 88*
index cards, 33, 41, 46, *54*
index, compared with contents page, 66
index, use of, 71, 72
indexes, 20, 21, 28, 58, 66, 70, 71, 74, 82, 86, 99, 106, 112
information, accessing, 86
insects, 34–41, 46–53, *67,* 71–80
instructions, 34, 46, 70, 74, 78, 79, 82, 90, 94
introductions, 58, 66, 70, 78

j

journals, 72, 103
Jupiter, *103*
justifying with reference to the text, 46

k

key (to map), 82, 98, *100,* 101

l

labelled diagrams, 20, 23, 38, 58, *59,* 66, *69,* 75, 78, *80,* 82, 86, 106, 112, *114*
landforms, 111
legend (key) to map, 82, 98, *100,* 101
letters (mail), 65, 88, 102
library catalogue, 97
lichens, 111
Life of the Butterfly, The, 20, 26, *28,* 37, 47, 52, 57, 68, **70-73,** 74, 76, 93, 97
Life of the Butterfly, The frieze, 10, *11,* 23, **70-71**
life cycle diagrams, *28,* 76
life cycles, **70-81**
life-size drawings, 77, 81
lift-the-flap books, *35,* 42–45

light, *97*, 111
liquids, 110
lists, 20, 23, 64, 94, 107, *115*
lists of predictions, 82
lists of questions to investigate, 82
lists, as basis for research, 113
lizards, *38*, *69*
logs, 103
lungs, *88*

m

magazines, as resource for research, 96
magnification, 95
magnifying containers, use of, 78
magnifying lenses, use of, 18, 22, 34, 37, 47, *75*, 92, 95
mammals, 43, 44
"map", meaning of, 101
map making, 42, **99-101**, *100*
map, world, *122*
mapping, 99–101
mapping, classroom, 101
mapping, local, 100
maps, *19*, 20, 42, 58, 60, 107, 112, *114*, *115*
maps, blank, 98
maps, color coding on, 101
maps, compared with aerial views, 100, *101*
maps, compared with globes, 99
maps, comparing, 114
maps, computer-generated, *113*
maps, including pictures, 36, 41
maps, key (legend) to, 82, 98, *100*, 101
maps, labelling of, 42
maps, political, 98
maps, radar, 106, *110*
maps, scale on, 101
maps, street, 98, *100*
maps, world, 99, *122*
Mars, *104*, *110*
marsupials, 44
mass, 59, 60, 62
matching, 25
matching information, 37
materials, 90–93
mathematics, *19*, 36, *53*, 59, 73, 76
mathematics problems, 59, 62
measuring distance, *68*
measuring height, *59*, 60, 68
measuring mass, *59*, 60
measuring size, 36, 60, *61*, 73, 76, 77, 81
media, electronic, 108
medical vocabulary, 83
Mercury, 107, 108, *111*
meteorology, 108
microclimate, 114
microscopes, use of, 18, 84, 92, 95, 96
Milky Way, *99*
Millions of Years Ago, **30-33**, 41, 81, 111
minerals, 90–93, 96
misleading graphs, 63
modelling note-taking, 34, 38, 93, 102
modelling research methods, 66, 97, 102
molecule, *89*
Moon, *105*
moths, 76–77, *93*
movement, 67–68, 84
muscles, *83*, *84*

museum, 32
"mystery facts," as a focus for discussion, 72
"mystery facts," as a writing model, 76
Mystery Monsters, *21*, 22, *25*, **34-37**, 41, 49, 51, 52, 56, 57, 69, 73, 77, 93

n

narrative, 26, 74, 79, 102, *104–105*
narrative, as stimulus for research, 104
Neptune, *105*, *109*
Neptune, moons of, 26
nerves, 85, *89*
news media, 104–105
news reports, scanning of, 114–115
newspaper articles, 114–115
newspaper conventions, 102, *103*, 104–105, *114*
newspapers, *103*, 114–115
night sky, 98, 105, 122, *130*, *131*
nonfiction big books, *see* "big books"
nonfiction conventions, 80
nonfiction, can be accessed through index, 72
nonfiction, choosing what we read in, 66
nonfiction, used to answer questions, 79
note-taking, *10*, 21
note-taking, modelling of, 34, 38, 93, 102
notes, 102
numbers, large, 30, 89
nutrition, 62–65

o

observing, 23
observing animals, 70–81
observing children, **28**
omnivores, 64
optical illusions, 56
oral language, 28, *see also* "discussion," "talk"
oral reports, 39
outdoor investigation, 39, 47, 50
ozone layer, 113

p

paintings, *107*
pairs, working in, 37, 40, 44, 46, 50, *see also* "small groups"
pets, 50, 64
photographs, 20, 38, 91, 106
photographs, as resource for discussion, 75, 89
photographs, as resource for writing, 47
photographs, close-up, 70, 74, 78
photographs, compared with diagrams, *66*, *67*
photographs, comparing, *104–105*
photographs, high-magnification, 34, 46
photographs, high-speed, 66, *69*
photographs, interpretation of, 112
photographs, labelled, 42
photographs, microscopic, 46, 86–89, 90–97
photographs, sequential, 70
photographs, x-ray, 86, 87
photography, 96, *105*
physical education, 67–68
pictograms, 62, 63, *65*

pictorial tables, 62
picture maps, 36, 41
"picture talk," use of, 30, 31, 98
pictures as summaries, *30–31*
pictures, as stimulus for discussion, 87
pie charts, 74, 80
planets, 98–111
plants, 90–93, *92, 97*
pollution, *113*
postcards, 21, 32, *85,* **102-105**
Postcards from the Planets, 19, 21, 23, 26, 32, 75, 93, 101, **102-105**, 109
posters, 56
predators, 36, *67, 73*
predicting information, 58
predicting pattern of text, 20
predicting words in the index, 74
predicting, using book title, 38
predicting, using cover picture and blurb, 34, 38, 82
prediction, using illustrations, *67*
predictions, justifying, *25*
predictions, refined by discussion, *38*
prehistory, **30-33**
prior knowledge, 21–22, 39
prior knowledge, evaluation of, 68
prior knowledge, list of, 107
problems, solving, 22, **24**, 34, 59, 62
puns, 65
puzzles, as stimulus for research, 21, 22, 24, 34, 59, 62, 89, 94, 95

q

questions and answers, 34, 38, 42, 46, 50, 70, *73, 80,* 86, *87,* 94, 98, 106
questions, constructing, 26, 32, 59, 68, 92, 96, 103, 112–113

r

radar, *110*
radio, 108
rainbows, 111
rainforests, 114
reading, 10
reading development, 20
reading level, 8
reading practice, 39
reading with a partner, 46, 50 *see also* "pairs, working in"
reading, purpose for, 23
recycling, 113, 115
reference books, 32, 40, 41
reference books, modelling use of, 81
repetitive page structure, 70, 90, 94
repetitive text structure, 20, 38, 46, 50, 57, 62, 98
reporting to the class, 39
reptiles, 32, 44, 88
research, 10, *18,* 22, **26-27**, *see also* "questions, constructing"
research, by writing to experts, 63
research, library, 26, 39, 50, 55, 56
research, modelling of, 97, 102
research, purpose for, 34
research, using magazines, 37
research, using pictures, 51
researching "three important facts," 36
retelling, *see* "transferring . . ."
revisiting the text, 31, 33, 45
rewriting, *see* "transferring . . ."
rhyme, 50, 57
role play, 31, 115
role play, as an aid to comprehension, 98
rough drafts, 51
rules, 37

S

Saturn, 103
scale diagrams, 58, 66, 68, 70, 72, *73,* 78
scale drawings, comparing, 73
scale, on maps, 101
scanning the text, 20, *see also* "skimming the text"
schedules, 62
science, **23**, **24**
scientific vocabulary, 83
seals, *65*
senses, 57, 85
sequencing pictures, 11, 79
sequential diagrams, 78, *80,* 100, 106, 111
sequential photographs, 70
shared experience, 20
shared reading, 20, *see also* "big books"
sharing information, 22
sharks, *65*
silhouette diagrams, 30, 60, *107*
size, 36, 60, *61,* 73, 76, 77, 81
skeletons, **42-45**, **82-85**
Skeletons, 24, 35, 41, **42-45**, 61, 65, 69, 76, 85, 89, 90, 93, 106
skimming the text, 20, 36, 86, 99
skin, 84
skull, *23,* 43, 84
Small Worlds, 20, 30, 41, 47, 57, 87, 88, 93, 101, 103, 105, **106-111**, 115
small books, 11, 26, 27
small books, for browsing, 58, 106
small books, for reading in pairs, 35, 58
small books, for reference, 103, 105
small books, for research, 87
small books, used in small groups, 54–55
small books, used to make a glossary, 69
small books, used to rewrite text, 80
small groups, 28, 33, *44, see also* "pairs, working in"
smog, 111
snake, scales of, *92*
solar energy, 110, 113
solar system, 98–111
solids, 110
Somewhere in the Universe, **98-101**, 105
space, 98–111
species, 45
spectrum, 111
speech bubbles, 50, *55,* 57, 62
speed, 67
spiders, 50
stars, 98, *130, 131*
storyboards, *33*
styles, comparing, 79
summaries, 42
summarizing, 27, 28, *30*
Sun, 98
symmetry, *49, 123*

t

tables, 20, 42, 50, 52, 64, 67, *68*, 71, 72, *73*, 74, *76*, 78, *80*, 85, 102, 106
tables, as summaries, *108*
tables, as writing models, 76
tables, children's, 81
tables, composed of real objects, *93*
tables, design of, *108*
tables, pictorial, 62
tables, used for classification, *93*
tables, used to evaluate prior knowledge, 68, 70
Tadpole Diary, 47, 49, 68, 69, 72, 74, 77, **78-81**, 97, 103
Tadpole Diary frieze, *11*, 79
tadpoles, **78-81**
talk, 10, 21, 22, 23, *38*, 40, 46, 80, 90–91, *92*
taste, sense of, 24, 85
"teachable moment," 77
technical terms, 17
technology, *97*
teeth, *23*, 43, 84
telescopes, use of, 96
temperature, 108, 109, 110, *114*, 115
temperature diagrams, 106
terrarium, use of, 114
text and graphics, comparing, 107
text, concealment of, 112
texts, compared with children's research, 80
texts, comparing, 30, 32, 36, 41, 67, 92
thermometer, use of, 109, 110
third person text, 92
time, *30*, 62, 67, 77, 108
time lines, 20, *30*, 31, 105
time travel, 32
title pages, 46, 62, 82, 91, *113*
tongue, *83*, 85
touch, sense of, 85
transferring diagrams into text, 84
transferring diary into expository text, 75
transferring graphics into text, 62
transferring photographs into text, 79
transferring picture and caption into text, *32*, 47, 82
transferring puzzles into expository text, *95*
transferring tables into expository text, 72
transferring text into a table, 73, 76, *108*
transferring text into diagrams, 20–21
transportation, 115
travel diaries, use of, 75
trees, 113
TV, 108

u

universe, 98–101
Uranus, *109*

v

Venn diagrams, *44*, *52*
Venus, 108, 109, *111*
viruses, *88*
vision, 56
visual clues, 54, 56

visual information, 20, 112
vitamins, *97*
vivarium, used to develop language, 70
vocabulary, 10, 83
vocabulary development, 83
vocabulary lists, made during discussion, 38
volcanic action, 111
volcanoes, *107*, *110*

w

wallcharts, *see* "friezes"
weather, 63, 108
weather forecasts, 108
weather reports, 106, 108
whales, *83*
What Did You Eat Today? 20, *25*, 41, 45, 49, 61, **62-65**, 68, 85, 93
What Is It? 22, 24, 26, 35, 41, 57, 65, 73, 77, 85, 89, 91, 92, 93, **94-97**.
wings, *83*
wolf, skull of, *23*
work folders, 28
work samples, **28**
writing, 10
writing a glossary, 81, 87
writing addresses, 98, 102, 103, 104
writing advertisements, 114
writing captions, *113*
writing diaries, 89, 103
writing expository text, *96*
writing from different points of view, 80
writing generalizations, *96*
writing guessing cards, 89
writing letters, 88, *103*
writing postcards, *103*, 104
writing recommendations for action, 114
writing the date, 102, 104
writing, extending the text, 31

x

x-ray photographs, 86, 87
x-rays, *83*, *87*

y

years and days, 108

z

zoos, 39, 51, **62-65**